Under the Gaijin Gaze: Essays on the Education & Attitudes of Japanese College Women

UNDER THE GAIJIN GAZE: ESSAYS ON THE EDUCATION
AND ATTITUDES OF JAPANESE COLLEGE WOMEN

Under the Gaijin Gaze: Essays on the Education & Attitudes of Japanese College Women

Daniel A. Metraux

Writers Club Press

San Jose New York Lincoln Shanghai

Under the Gaijin Gaze: Essays on the Education & Attitudes of
Japanese College Women

Writers Club Press
an imprint of iUniverse.com, Inc.

For information address:
iUniverse.com, Inc.
5220 S 16th, Ste. 200
Lincoln, NE 68512
www.iuniverse.com

ISBN: 0-595-19405-2

Printed in the United States of America

I wish to dedicate this work to close friends who in recent years have brought so much joy to my life: Jim McCrory, Mike Gentry, Dianne Mason, Bob Grotjohn, Doug Clark, John Wells, Nancy and Lewis Hill, Richard Zuckerman, Megumi Okura, Noriko Okura, Ron Lovelace, Rod Owen, Marion Ward, Ben and Tomoko Dorman, and Rick Plant. Also my wonderful departmental colleagues: Anne McGovern, Martha Walker, Carrie Douglass, Ivy Arbulu, and Stephens Garlick.

Contents

Section I

Education

Japanese women are Japan's hidden resource. They are well educated, highly disciplined, and willing to work long and hard. Yet, at a time when Japan's population is about to decline so rapidly that Japan's major corporations will face a severe shortage of young talented male leadership, the nation's leadership elite is virtually ignoring the contributions that young women could make to fill the gap.

This problem is made more severe by the reluctance of women to take the initiative to take their place among Japan's leaders. The fault lies with the still widely held assumption that women are secondary citizens who hold a servile position in society. The higher educational system for women compounds the problem by educating them specifically for their traditional roles and not giving them the specialized training needed for leadership in a highly technological society. Women perpetuate the problem by accepting their secondary status and not considering professional careers except in very isolated cases.

The purpose of this book is to present a portrait of the lives and attitudes of female college students in Japan and to demonstrate how women's education fails to prepare them adequately for a meaningful role in Japanese society.

The final section of the book takes the problem one step further to examine how the nation's high-profile JET program has failed to improve the quality of language and intercultural education in Japan.

This research on Japanese women and higher education through the eyes of my 230 students at KWC and of four former Mary Baldwin College students who were simultaneously working in Japanese schools as teachers in the Japanese government-sponsored JET (Japanese Exchange Teacher) Program.

I spent the 1999-2000 academic year teaching in the English Department of a prestigious women's college in Kyoto with the goal of learning more about Japan's educational system from the inside and, more importantly, to get a closer look at Japan's younger generation. I had already lived in Japan for four years over a series of earlier visits dating from 1968, but I had always come as a student, researcher, or guide for groups of American students. Although I was a guest professor at a university near Tokyo for a semester in 1992 and had visited the Kyoto school over several summers in the 1990s, the 1999-2000 faculty appointment was my first time actually inside of the Japanese system.

I have employed a fictional name, Kansai Women's College [KWC], for the university where I taught in 1999-2000.

This work is limited in its scope to the lives of the largely middle-class female students at KWC. We will analyze their educational system through their own eyes and amplify their individualism by soliciting their views on a variety of issues including marriage, politics and society, international relations, and their country's future. Their lives are in some respects different from the majority of young Japanese who attend co-educational colleges or who don't attend college and who may have a very different perspective on life. For this reason, I have included material from various popular Japanese weekly magazines as *SPA!* to provide a broader perspective on Japanese youth. I have also thrown in elements of my own experience as a teacher in Japan to portray both the frustrations as well as the many joys of a *gaijin* (foreign) teacher at a Japanese university.

Kansai Women's College is a vital part of a "family" of schools that includes primary and secondary schools as well as mainstream co-educational University. The Women's College and mainstream University share an old adjoining campus in downtown Kyoto that dates from the 1870s and an ultra-modern adjoining campus in suburban Kyoto between Kyoto and Nara. Both campuses maintain separate areas for the Women's College and the main university with very separate faculties and administrators and students in one school cannot take courses in the other.

The University and Women's College are considered the strongest private educational institutions not only in the Kansai region, but in all of western Japan. KWC has approximately 5000 students who study in five faculties: English (the most Popular), Japanese, Music, Home Economics, and Contemporary Society.[1] A once-flourishing junior college graduated its last class in 2001.

My official title at KWC was "Contract Teacher," but I taught a full slate of courses and was assigned 24 freshman junior-college students as advisees. My nine classes several English conversation, composition and advanced writing classes as well as advanced courses in American culture and Japanese Religion.[2]

My goal in each class was to train and encourage my students to express their own opinions in English on a variety of issues. Students in conversation classes had to make weekly speeches in English while those in writing classes wrote 1-2 page weekly essays on similar questions. Advanced students wrote 10-15 page term papers on select issues each semester as well as weekly essays.

---

[1] This new department (*gendai shakai*), which opened in April 2000, embraces a variety of special fields including business management, careers in tourism, computers, and sociology. The goal is to expand the offerings for young women whose career horizons are entering many new domains in Japanese society.

[2] The religion course included 12 foreign students from the United States, Canada and New Zealand.

During my year-long appointment, I myself wrote a weekly journal to a number of friends and colleagues analyzing the student's views. This work draws from these journal entries as well as from subsequent interviews with my Japanese students. I have attempted to maintain as much of the freshness and immediacy of these journals as well as many direct quotations from the students' essays.

This work is divided into four sections. Part I is an analysis of the students' attitudes towards education as well as a more general commentary on the state of higher education in Japan. The second section examines the students' views on a variety of social and political issues facing Japan, while the third part looks at their views on matters concerning war and peace. Part IV looks at the Japanese government's ambitious JET program from the perspective of three young American teachers who present their views on Japanese education and their students. The Conclusion section seeks to place the diverse essays into greater perspective concerning the lives of young women college students in Japan.

THE GAIJIN PROFESSOR IN JAPAN

Thirty years ago when I first entered graduate school in the Dept. of East Asian Languages and Cultures at Columbia University, my Japanese professor and mentor Ichiro Shirato sternly warned his students against the easy temptation of taking an English teaching job at any Japanese university. At that time Americans or other English-speaking graduate students with advanced degrees could land a very well paying job fairly easily at a notable Japanese university. Prof. Shirato warned us to be wary of such positions—we would be inundated with work that had little to do with our scholarly training and we would receive little or no respect in American academic circles.

I followed Prof Shirato's advice and have built a career in teaching and research at Mary Baldwin College. But coming to Japan to teach at a major

Japanese university for a year permitted me a glimpse of the life of the *gaijin sensei*. My experiences reminded me somewhat of a group of *gaijin* who had taught at Japanese academies and universities a century earlier.

During the late 1860s and early 1870s Japan's new Meiji government began the revolutionary process of rapidly opening and modernizing Japan. The government realized that education had to be the key to its success and mobilized its resources to build a modern educational system encompassing all young Japanese. Primary schools were built in every village, and hundreds of secondary schools and the foundations for various universities were begun. The central and various regional and local governments began to hire a number of young or slightly older experts and teachers from the United States and Europe to assist in this modernization process.

One of my current research projects involves the study of the career of E. Warren Clark (1849-1907), a then 23-year-old American who came to Japan to teach the family and neighbors of the deposed Tokugawa shoguns who hoped to use education as a means to regain power. Clark taught science and English in Shizuoka before the Japanese government transferred him to the Kaisei Gakkoo (now Tokyo University) to set up a new chemistry department. He had a whopping salary of $3600 a year in gold—perhaps over $80-90,000 in today's money throughout his stay in Japan.

The method of education was ingenious. The school building had many lab rooms, over 1,000 students, but only one main teacher, Clark. Clark would spend the morning lecturing to a group of 30-40 Japanese teaching assistants who had a good command of English. The TAs took careful notes and each delivered the same lecture to about 25 younger students in English and Japanese in the afternoon. That way Clark could actually teach science intensively to 1,000 students every day. After about 14 months of hard study the 1000 students graduated and many if not most became science teachers in primary and secondary schools across Japan.

Clark left Shizuoka after 14 months and became the first teacher in the new chemistry department at Tokyo University. Clark wrote of his admiration and devotion to his students—he had never imagined that young people could work so hard and learn so much so quickly. He also greatly admired Japan, but remarked constantly how lonely he was. The Japanese were most courteous and friendly, he noted, but he received few invitations, and he had to turn to the growing American community in Japan for real friendship. He commended school authorities for their courteous behavior towards him. He advised that to succeed in Japan a foreigner must work hard, keep a very low profile, and rarely if ever complain. This remains good advice that every foreigner in Japan should heed.[3]

The Japanese are still importing tens of thousands of foreigners to teach them English as well as a host of other skills. KWC is more successful than some at recruiting foreign teachers because of its insistence that virtually every English class be taught by a native speaker who is trained to teach foreigners. Each year, KWC employs perhaps 7-8 full time North

---

[3] E. Warren Clark described his teaching in remote Shizuoka Prefecture in 1871-73 in his book, *Life and Adventure in Japan* (New York: American Tract Society, 1878). He lived in a beautiful old Buddhist temple and would spend Sunday, his only day off, by the shore looking east towards his homeland (pp. 50-52)

Earthquakes, robbers, and the romantic experiences of a strange country kept life in the old Buddhist temple free from the monotony for some time; but at last it became very lonely, as the romance and novelty faded out, and the clatter of drums and gongs in the temple, instead of being musical, became intolerable. I used to wander up through the woods, passing the Buddhist burying ground, and sit down on top of the hill (on every Sabbath afternoon), and look across the Pacific towards home.

The sullen roar of the ocean could be heard as the waves broke heavily upon the beach five miles away; that same sea washed the shores of my own country, nearly five thousand miles further east. The sun set over the western hills of Japan, and reappeared rising from the ocean, fresh from its journey across the continent of America. It came to me bright and cheery every morning from "home," though all my distant friends were in bed and asleep in America at the time it reached me in Japan.

Americans or other native English speakers who teach English language and content courses. Their salaries rival those of Clark and, like him, they are skilled practitioners who fulfill a very necessary need in Japanese higher education. They teach 6-8 courses and are inundated with committee and other administrative work which leaves virtually no time for research. In addition to this full-time contingency of foreign instructors, there are two temporary contract teachers such as myself who teach 9 courses, but who have no committee work. Our salaries are correspondingly lower, but "below" us in the professional hierarchy are perhaps several dozen part-timers who teach up to three courses on campus one-or-two days a week. They too are skilled practitioners who want to survive in Japan, but they must teach at perhaps 3-4 *different* colleges a week, making altogether perhaps 1/3 or 1/4 what my full-time colleagues make. Nevertheless, they hang on for years, mostly marrying Japanese, hoping perhaps to land a full-time post.

Still the days and months rolled by, and though I worked hard and kept busy, there were hours when the sense of loneliness seemed too oppressive to be borne. On the Sabbath especially I would pace to and fro on my temple porch, or climb alone to the hill-top, and think of the long months yet to come before I could hope to see a familiar face or hear a familiar American voice.

If I could only see a single foreigner like myself for "just a few minutes," I would often say, then I thought I would be happy and willing to stand another siege of seclusion from society. But when this did happen eventually, and two friends came all the way from Yokohama to visit me for a few days, I felt all the more lonely after they left; for the solitude seemed more complete, in contrast to the merry social times which they said everybody was having in Yokohama and Tokio. Nevertheless, I believe in solitude, and I like it, provided it comes in doses that can be endured. I believe that true development comes through some form of solitude faster than through most forms of society. One can be happy alone, if he has the proper resources within himself; and I look back upon that old Buddhist temple as the brightest and happiest spot that I have yet seen in the world.

The high salaries do come at a price. Foreign teachers throughout the system are tapped for their skills, but very little attention is paid to them as people. The Japanese will tolerate you if you work hard and are useful, but theirs is a most homogenous society that does little to welcome even the most seasoned Japan-hand. Unless you cultivate your own friends, both foreign and Japanese, it can be a lonely and solemn life. One American teacher at a Japanese college remarked bitterly that in 15 years of teaching in Japan, he had gone out with Japanese colleagues on only two occasions.

One of my former MBC students now working for JET, Tarah Blazek, once noted that foreigners with close ties in their home country (boy friends, family, etc) will be miserable in Japan. Those without such ties or who wish to escape a life back home have a chance to flourish in Japan.

If one is strong and up to the challenge, a foreign teacher in Japan can make good money, have a wide variety of Japanese and international friends, and travel cheaply to other parts of Asia during vacation periods. But if one is shy and misses ties with home, life in Japan can be pure Hell.

A CRISIS IN EDUCATION

Japan today is experiencing a relentless recession that began in the early 1990s and shows no signs of abating a decade later. Because the causes of this crisis are highly complex, its resolution will involve many varied factors. A critical concern that might provoke further economic problems is a projected decline in population: the proportion of young people and active members of the work force will be reduced while the number of elderly Japanese skyrockets.

This projected decline of Japan's labor force means that there may be far fewer managers and workers than necessary to participate in the expansion of the nation's economy and to support the growing pool of nonproductive retirees. There are, however, two possible remedies that could greatly increase the number of productive workers: increased immigration and better use of women in the work force.

Immigration could bring many young intelligent workers from Korea, China and other Asian countries, but Japan's pronounced ethnocentricity would make it difficult to accept vast numbers of permanent residents from abroad. Japan's other hidden resource, its well-educated young women, could also find a more fulfilling role as admini- strators and exec- utives in government and business.

Today Japanese women are making many gains in terms of education, independence, and social choice, but they continue to face real discrimi- nation in terms of employment. Many large corporations have two hiring tracks: an executive course for well-educated males and a support track of more temporary female workers. Even female graduates of elite universi- ties face huge hurdles in their efforts to enter the executive sections of major corporations and businesses.

Discrimination, however, is only one of several factors that inhibit the advancement of women in business and professional life in contemporary Japan. The sad fact is that, at present, young Japanese women lack both the training and self-confidence to achieve leadership positions in society. Very few young Japanese women have a worldview that encompasses lead- ership roles or professional careers. Rather, an overwhelming majority look forward to jobs as Office Ladies (Ols) for a few years before enter- taining matrimony.

The greater tragedy is that Japan's educational system perpetuates the secondary and passive role of women. Although women receive the same primary and secondary educations as men, there is a definite bifurcation in Japan's higher educational systems. Men go to larger colleges and uni- versities that offer a wide variety of programs of study and key links to jobs in industry and government.

Most women, however, go to junior colleges or women's colleges that offer a far narrower range of programs of study. One of the most popular majors at women's colleges is English, but female students can also choose to study music, Japanese, food science or other related majors. These programs train women for jobs as OLs, but not for professional careers. The focus is on learning practical skills or "liberal arts" courses that will develop "lady-like" qualities, but little professional training.

While increasing numbers of women are attending larger colleges and universities with men, they remain a distinct minority. Most women still seek admittance to junior colleges or women's colleges that offer a very safe and traditional track to OL jobs and eventual matrimony.

Modern Japan is experiencing a revolution of youth culture. Although its social institutions and educational system are still structured for a more traditional Japan in which consensus, group behavior, and male dominance still dominate society, but where the younger generation seeks to carve a very different niche. Today's youth focuses more on individualism, equality, and self-gratification. Young Japanese want to develop their own lives and pursue fulfilling careers that go well beyond their country's traditional corporate culture.

Many young Japanese are moving from the traditional norms of harmony and consensus. Many are out for thrills, not wanting anything to do with the button-downed uniform lives of their parents. Many seem to be crafting their own unique styles, pursuing an unfocused commitment to do things differently in a society that stresses conformity and politeness. For example, many dye their hair in varying shades of garish color and tan their skins to resemble California lifeguards. They kiss each other passionately and jabber loudly on their cell handyphones in public while sprawled across the floors of packed trains. In some cases, they even cause trouble: there is a juvenile crime wave spreading across Japan and a number of teenage girls from middle-class families prostitute themselves for middle-aged men. Some primary and secondary schools once famous for rigidity and discipline have evolved into chaotic places where even teachers are assaulted on occasion.

One of the causes of the current unrest among young Japanese is the country's archaic educational system which in many ways is failing the very people it is supposed to serve. The emphasis is still on discipline and information when younger Japanese are seeking greater creativity and individualism. Universities that provided corporate and bureaucratic Japan with its silent salarymen soldiers remain solidly glued to the curricula of the past.

The main stumbling block to necessary reform is the conservative bloc that dominates the government and governing boards of universities. It is sad that Japanese universities have not moved sufficiently from their traditional role of catering to corporate Japan to serving the needs of Japanese youth. This conservative approach is enhanced by entrenched bureaucrats in the Ministry of Education who have spent much of the postwar period trying to roll back the liberal reforms brought in under the American occupation. These same bureaucrats have stated that the Occupation reforms put too much emphasis on the individual and not enough on the citizen's duties to the state.

As members of this restless generation, young women today have far more liberal attitudes concerning their personal and social lives; for instance, more young women now assume the right to determine whom they will marry and when and where the ceremony will take place. Compared to their mothers and grandmothers Japanese women have achieved considerable freedom to manage and direct their own personal lives, but concerning their working lives and perceptions of their career potential, they still remain where they were a generation or more ago. They rarely conceive of the possibility of pursuing a professional career or administrative rank in a company or government office.

Women could play a dynamic and leading role in Japan's rapidly evolving technological economy. They could fill the gaps that will appear when there are not enough young Japanese men available to manage and develop this new economy. To do so however, they must overcome two substantial barriers: men's biases and their own lack of training and self-confidence.

JAPAN'S CRISIS IN HIGHER EDUCATION FOR WOMEN

Japan has a well-earned reputation for its success in developing a highly effective system of primary and secondary education, but Japanese higher education at both the undergraduate and graduate levels is often quite deficient and in many cases does little to prepare young women, in particular, for life in a modern, highly technological society. Organizational, structural, and philosophical reforms are necessary if Japanese universities are to provide the diversity and the analytical training necessary for women to advance in Japanese society. Currently, Women are trained only as generalists with practical skills that would serve them well as secretaries or administrative assistants, but Japanese women's colleges provide virtually no background in leadership, science and technology, or managerial preparation and little training in those specialized areas to prepare women for a professional life. Women's colleges in Japan, whatever their prestige, amount to little more than glorified finishing schools whose graduates may work in subordinate positions for a few years, but who eventually leave work to support a "salaryman" husband and to raise his children.

There is a vast difference between the curriculum found at a major co-educational university in Japan and that of a major women's college. Co-educational universities offer a diverse curriculum that includes the natural and social sciences. Graduate wings offer programs in a variety of fields and the academic programs at some of these schools, especially in medicine and the sciences, can be quite good. The number of women attending these schools is rising, but males still predominate by a healthy margin.

Kansai Women's College offers its 5000 students a far narrower range of programs. Three thousand students major in English, studying where they study English language and culture. When they graduate, they are proficient in English, but have very other few practical skills or training in any other fields. Smaller numbers of students focus on music, Japanese, or food science. A new grouping of courses in business administration, social work, Kyoto tourism and the like offers some practical training for jobs in the business world. On the other hand, KWC offers no courses in math, natural science, many of the social sciences, and little attention to computers. A handful of these students study abroad to gain access to more variety, but their numbers have declined drastically over the past decade due primarily to Japan's enduring recession.

The courses of study offered here are either narrowly utilitarian or broadly ephemeral, but they have little connection with Japan's highly technical and science-based economy. A major in music is very pleasing to the ear, but few if any of the graduates go on to become professional musicians. Students of the Japanese department may become teachers, but generally these students of the weakest department on campus settle for mediocre positions as "office ladies" (Ols) in regional companies. Graduates of the English Department may get better jobs, but unless they have studied abroad their command of English is embarrassingly weak and their jobs tend to be supportive of the male hierarchy. The new curriculum that includes tracks in business management and Kyoto tourism is a step in the right direction, but they remain very utilitarian, doing little to train women for positions of executive leadership.

One very positive element of KWC is that it does hire a large staff of well-trained foreign teachers, mainly American, who provide both exposure to a foreign culture, good training in language skills, and demanding courses. There are also a number of Japanese faculty who have received some undergraduate or graduate training abroad and also provide some good training for their students. But these professors are hampered by a system that forces students to take too many courses simultaneously and leaves too little time to study adequately in any one course.

Ironically, despite all this foreign contact, students at KWC, like so many of their counterparts in the United States, have very little understanding of the world outside Japan. Primary and secondary students learn little if anything about the world beyond their nation's borders. Very few male Japanese study abroad during college and thus enter the corporate world with very little understanding of the dynamics of foreign cultures. Tens of thousands of Japanese women study in American, Australian, Canadian, or other Asian colleges every year, and some return to promising jobs in industry, communications and government; yet their career tracks are more support-oriented than leader- ship-oriented.

Japan has experienced a lengthy recession since the early 1990s that defies the efforts of the government and big business to bring about a resurgence of economic growth. One long-range solution would be a true commitment to reforms that encompass a break from the highly regulated economic practices of the past and that place more emphasis on entrepreneurship and individual initiative. One detriment to such a scenario is the failure of Japanese education, especially at higher levels, to emphasize creativity and independence, especially among women. Japanese are taught the arts of hard work and discipline in primary and secondary school, but they will be hard pressed to bloom once again as a people and a nation without a stronger sense of independence.

Japanese Ministry of Education (*mombusho*) officials are very aware of this problem. A leading Mombusho official told a *New York Times* reporter that "Our current system, just telling our kids to study, study, study has been a failure. Endless studying worked in the past when there were many kids in the school system. Japan was rebuilding and the competition was very fierce. But that is no longer the case, and the kids are far fewer, things are not as competitive anymore, and just telling them to study more will no longer work."[4]

Many educators in Japan share a growing concern that their orderly but unimaginative school system excels at producing pliant, disciplined workers, which the nation needed after World War II, but is failing to produce

---

[4] Howard W. French, "More Sunshine for Japan's Overworked Students" in *The New York Times*, 25 February 2001.
http://www.nytimes.com/2001/02/25/world/25JAPA.html
[5] Ibid.

the problem solvers and innovators needed for the future, especially among women.[5]

A radical decline in younger Japanese and in college applicants has only served to compound the problem. Japan's 18-year-old population has fallen by roughly 25 percent since the 1992 peak, and so university applicants have decreased by an equal percentage over the past decade. Because there has been very little change in the number of students each school can admit, schools are lowering their admissions standards, thereby allowing the average scholastic level of students to markedly decline.[6] Kansai Women's College, for example, used to be very competitive even a few years ago, but in the Spring of 2000 it was admitting ten out of every eighteen applicants, and many faculty complained vigorously over the decreasing caliber of their younger students.

This writer has long taught Japanese female students at various colleges in the United States with excellent results. Japanese students who study abroad are a self-selecting group of achievers who are willing to work hard to master material in a foreign language. They make huge financial and personal sacrifices because of their belief that their lives and careers can be enhanced through study in the West. They are often rewarded with challenging and successful careers when they return to Japan because they have had the opportunity to specialize in fields they could never study at home and because they have learned to assert themselves as individuals.

Teaching in Kyoto for 1999-2000 brought a very different view of Japanese higher education and a better understanding of why so many Japanese long to study abroad. It was clear that some learning was going on, that some professors led excellent classes, and that a number of hard working students were profiting from the system.

---

[6] Kiyonari Tadao, "Talking Business: University Challenge" in *Look Japan* (March 2001), p. 18.

On the other hand, I encountered hundreds of students at KWC who were getting at best a hollow education. They attended classes taught by largely disinterested teachers who provided the students with limited amounts of interesting and useful material to study. A number of foreign, largely American, teachers had a strong following as did some of the Japanese faculty, but students bitterly complained about the many Japanese teachers who taught them in a haughty and boring manner and about the need to take so many courses that they often could not distinguish between one and another.

Another occasional complaint was that Kansai Women's College was simply failing to prepare its students for careers (as opposed to jobs) in a highly technological economy. KWC students in the English Department were certainly developing sound English skills, but one must know far more than just English for a genuine career. Even with the addition of a new faculty that trains students for careers in tourism or business management, the college still does nothing to prepare its students for professional careers in the sciences, law, medicine, journalism and the like.

Women in Japan become almost automatic second-class citizens because supposedly prestigious Japanese universities treat their women with a degree of benign contempt. It is hardly surprising that few women graduates go on to prestigious careers when their educational institutions have prepared them to be glorified office clerks or educated mothers with few real prospects for a successful professional life.

This phenomenon, superficial education, is hardly limited to just Japan. I have talked to dozens of undergraduate and graduate students from other Asian countries who tell the same story. A Korean graduate student at Florida State University related that she came to the United States because she realized that even though she was studying at a prestigious university in Seoul (Yonsei University), her training there was superficial at best.

MARRIAGE, CHILDREN AND JAPAN'S POPULATION TIME BOMB

Although almost 150 years have passed since Commodore Perry's "Black Ships" ended Japan's traditional *sakoku* policy that barred almost all foreigners from entering Japan and similarly prohibited Japanese from leaving the country, Japan today remains very hostile to immigration. It is almost impossible, for example, for a foreigner to acquire Japanese citizenship without marrying a Japanese. The tragedy is that Japan's modern version of *sakoku* could have devastating effects for the economic future of Japan.

The problem of the "population time bomb" is frequently discussed in Japan. If current fertility rates continue, the nation's population will begin to decline very rapidly after the year 2007. The current population of about 130 million will decline to 92 million in 2050 and 50 million in 2100 [Similar trends are predicted for Korea as well]. At the same time, Japan's population is rapidly aging, meaning that there is the potential for the work force (people aged 20-65) to decline even faster. Economic decline is a real possibility with a far smaller work force.

One of the critical problems is that women today are having far fewer babies and are marrying much later -if at all. According to the Asahi Evening News:[7]

"Japan is a difficult place for a woman to raise a child, partly because in practice this is a nation of single mothers. Husbands stagger home late from the office or a bar, and a government poll found that fathers spend an average of just six minutes a day looking after their children." Having children in contemporary Japan is also very stressful and expensive. One Japanese housewife noted: "I have a good office job and the last thing that I want is a child. Its really a matter of whether having a child is worth all

---

[7] *Asahi Evening News,* June 2, 1999, p. 1.

the stress and pressure. Besides, I get no help from my husband. He has the traditional idea that women should enjoy raising children. I've heard that men say they're staying at work late because going home early means having to take care of children."

Many of my students would dispute this house- wife's comments: they claim that they look forward to motherhood, but a healthy and growing minority would agree with her criticism. And it is this growing minority that will cause problems for Japan in the future. One obvious solution would be immigration. Today tens of thousands of Chinese are sneaking into Japan to take on dirty and dangerous jobs, but because some of the immigrants are gangsters, more Japanese are frightened than ever of large-scale immigration. Japanese people are horribly and deeply concerned about maintaining cultural and racial homogeneity and purity.

The Asahi Shimbun reports that:[8]

If Tokyo made an all-out effort, it could recruit many of the best young scholars and engineers from India, Taiwan, Vietnam and China to study and work in Japan. That could revitalize the economy and create a boom for entrepreneurship, but few in Japan seem enthusiastic about that idea, and many seem fatalistic about the waves of Asian migration that bypass Japan and continue on to the United States.

A former member of the Japanese Diet, Endo Otohiko, told me in July 1999 (when he was still in office) that immigration was definitely not the answer to Japan's population dilemma. He suggests that Japan must do everything to encourage fertility-tax breaks, cheaper and more accommodating day-care centers, education programs to encourage fathers to be better fathers (ie-changing diapers), etc. A fine idea perhaps, but nearly everybody who will be in Japan's labor force in 2025 is already born.

It is indeed ironic that Japan's concern for racial purity and its hostility to foreign immigration might doom the nation to political and

---

[8] Ibid.

economic insignificance in the not too distant future. But it is also true that the Japanese are a very pragmatic people who will do what they have to do to survive.

JAPANESE COLLEGES FIND FEWER STUDENTS

There was an ominous note on the bulletin board in the faculty common room at the college. Applications for the entrance exam for the English Department, which has a solid majority of the college's 5000 students, were down a whopping 25 percent in 2000 after a modest four percent decline last year. KWC is a good school with no fears for the immediate future, but a 25% decline *does* mean *lowering admission standards* to keep the same student body.

As noted elsewhere, Japan is facing a severe population problem—and an actual decline will begin in 2007. Women are getting married much later (most say they want to marry at 30 and a few say never), are working after marriage more, are having fewer babies (1.53 rate), and are getting divorced more often (1/3). Japan's colleges and universities expanded greatly a generation ago to meet the great postwar baby boom, but with few immigrants, the traditional college age group is shrinking rapidly - even though a higher percentage of young Japanese now attend college. Japan has made a few genuine efforts to attract students outside the traditional college-age group—few older adults return college — although many older Japanese tell me that they would welcome the opportunity should it exist.

KWC is rallying to change its student base before it crumbles—and is a high quality wealthy school that will survive. However other newer, less financially secure and less quality-based schools are either closing or girding themselves for severe problems in the near future. Today a rising number of schools are admitting virtually f not entirely anybody who applies.

Another development is that even the best, most famous schools, except, perhaps Tokyo University, are getting fewer test applicants which means that schools once almost totally beyond the reach of moderate students are suddenly clamoring for these lesser students—the quality base is certainly down.

WHAT DO YOUNG JAPANESE WOMEN REALLY KNOW?

While I was teaching in Japan during 1999-2000, a number of articles appearing in the Japanese press that challenged the intellectual ability of younger Japanese today, especially women.[9] The sentiment is that the nation has experienced an anti-intellectual trend in many sectors of society and that the nation's preoccupation with university entrance examinations prevents a meaningful education.

Educator Sawa Takamitsu writes:

In the early 1970s, when student movements sparked violent campus disputes, it was fashionable to read translations of philosophical foreign books such as those on French structuralism. After peace returned to the campus, however, new reactionary trends emerged: anti-intellectualism and the advocacy of neo-nationalism by rightist polemicists. At first glance, there seems to be no relationship between the "anti-intellectual revolution" and the intensification of the "examination wars." In reality, these are closely intertwined. The spread of anti-intellectual- ism killed high-school students' interest in philosophy and thought and gave children the illusion that cramming for entrance examinations is about the only intellectual activity. As a result senior high school students devoted themselves to cramming for universities.[10]

---

[9] See especially Takamitsu Sawa, "Cramming Cripples Japan," in *The Japan Times*, 18 October 1999, p. 16.

[10] Ibid.

My students in Kyoto complained bitterly that their memorization of endless facts about history and other fields was helpful only when they encountered college entrance exams and that deep studies of arcane English grammar were useless outside of the exam system. They unanimously stated that they had already forgotten most of the material that had been pumped into their brains as recently as 18 months before.

These students note that while they may know a lot of historical facts, they have no real understanding of the flow and meaning of history. To put it simply, they know the "what" of history, but are clueless over the "why." They know the facts about Pearl Harbor, but have no idea about its causes and results. They had never heard of Admiral Yamamoto and Kita Ikki, critically important Japanese leaders before and at the start of World War II.

Young Japanese, my students included, have very little training in "how to think"—how to come up with original ideas. This is a cliché that appears in many Western writings about Japanese education, but it is also true. It is sad that even my brightest freshmen in Kyoto were much less capable of logical and historical thinking than many of my students at Mary Baldwin. Some juniors and seniors learned to write good critical essays in English[11], but their knowledge and understanding of their own modern history as well as recent world history and current events is horrendous. The worldview of younger Japanese today is perhaps even more parochial than that of American college students.

Sawa concludes his essay:

The scholastic level of Japanese students has been declining at an alarming pace. If the trend continues, Japan will be reduced to a second-rate country even in the domain where it is traditionally strong:

---

[11] Several students stated that they much preferred the foreign professors because these teachers gave them the unique opportunity to express themselves..

manufacturing technology. The prospects for Japan in the postindustrial age—in which software ability holds the key to success—look even more dismal.[12]

Little is done to help the student in college. The average freshman at my college takes as many as 16-17 courses at the same time in order to accumulate enough credits to graduate. She is in class from early morning to early evening with only a brief lunch break. If she travels an average 90 minutes from home to school by train every day, she rises early and comes home late, too exhausted to do any serious study. She will certainly improve her English, but she never takes a meaningful social or natural science course and her ability to speak German or French after two years study is most sad.

Ultimately, however, it is the Japanese college graduate who suffers. She emerges crammed with much information, but little comprehension. When middle-aged Japanese are given tests concerning their understanding of math and science, they finish at the *bottom* or *near the bottom* among the major industrial nations of the world.[13] Their failures in history and current events make for an embarrassing joke.

This form of education is also tiring and numbing for teachers as well. I taught a high load of eight separate courses for nine 90-minute periods a week–the equivalent of a nine-course load. There was little time for proper preparation and grading of weekly essays prepared by my 230plus students and virtually no time to get to know them personally. I returned home very nervous and tired every night wondering if I had the physical stamina to survive.

A nine-course teaching load is a crushing burden. The average faculty member at my school not only teaches six yearlong courses, but also faces endless and exhauasting committee and faculty meetings. The total

---

[12] Sawa,, p. 16.
[13] Ibid.

drudgery of a Japanese professor's life leaves far too little room for creative thinking and scholarship. This deep fatigue lowers faculty productivity and scholarly output.

THE INSTRUCTIONAL PROCESS: TOO MUCH OF TOO LITTLE

There are many clichés that ring true about Japan. One of them is the saying: "Form over Substance." One may say that a critical problem with Japanese higher education is that what might look good on paper in reality has very little "meat." Students take a wide range of courses with very impressive-sounding titles, but the simple fact is that students are forced to take so many courses at once and teachers must teach so many slots that students have little or no time to study and teachers can do little to prepare. It is more a tragic farce than quality education.

When Japan developed its first modern universities in the late 19th century, the nation was racing to catch up with the West and avoid being colonized. Japanese leaders wanted technology and practical know-how, but not the West's liberal intellectual traditions. Most universities in Japan are still geared to mass-producing graduates who can cram facts, follow orders, and work impossibly long hours. That is what Japan Inc. wanted when manufacturing was king and the economy was booming.

Early in my stay at KWC I asked to see the full academic schedules of a group of my advisees. What I discovered was really shocking. My freshmen students were being worked to death, but I wondered if they were learning anything of substance.

The academic day at KWC is divided into four 90-minute periods plus two classes on Saturdays (eliminated in 2000). The average student has classes for 14-17 of these 22 periods. She arrives for class every morning at 9 AM and leaves no earlier than 5 PM. Except for a 50-minute lunch break, she is *always* in class. Each of these slots represents a class that meets only once a week. Even a basic language class like elementary French or Chinese (the most popular language after English) meets only once a week with an occasional added session for conversation. The classes generally last for two 12-week semesters.[14]

After a full year on the faculty, one of the Chinese teachers complained that the system did not permit him to teach effectively. He had met his class for only 22 90-minute sessions and had over 20 students in each class. There were a few extra conversation and review sessions, but he was convinced that few if any students could even carry on a basic conversation in Chinese. "This was very different than in China, where we take language study very seriously and where students studying Japanese demonstrate real progress. That is the real difference between Japanese and Chinese education."

There is much discussion concerning the effectiveness of the learning process in Japanese universities. I know many KWC graduates who ultimately receive a good education and get solid jobs, but for many the key to success is graduation from a good name school rather than the mastery of a skill or subject. If a student has 15-16 courses, arrives home at night totally exhausted after a two-hour commute each way, and spends 10-20 hours working part-time on the week-end, how can she study outside the classroom?

A professor in Japan learns to give short homework assignments to get effective results. When I assigned short essays I would get excellent results. I also learned to use class time for writing and speaking assignments which was one way to insure that the students studied and put their studies to use. If you wanted to train your students to write, you devoted much of

---

[14] I have had many Japanese transfer students at MBC whose transcripts say that they have had two or four semesters of a foreign language, but who cannot even say a sentence in that language. Again, "Form over Substance."

class time to having them write an essay in class. By so doing, the teacher is assured that some progress is being made in the course.

I really wonder if students would learn more and faculty would teach better if they had a real US-style semester system in which faculty taught 3-4 courses and students took no more than 4-5 courses. Some Japanese colleges are now offering one-semester courses, but course loads remain high.

INEPTITUDE IN ENGLISH

The woes of college teaching in Japan are compounded by well-documented evidence that even though most Japanese take years of middle school or high-school English, young Japanese are fundamentally inept in the language. Some of my more advanced students, especially those who had lived abroad, showed some proficiency in English, but most of my freshmen and sophomores were very weak.

The Japanese government issued a report in early 2000 that made headlines with its proposal to make English the country's official second language. "Achieving world-class excellence requires a working knowledge of English." It called for reorganizing English classes according to level of achievement rather than grade, improving teacher training, increasing the number of foreign teachers, and contracting language schools that teach English.

The need for such action is clear, according to government officials, because Japan scores near the bottom of all Asian countries on the TOEFEL exam, the international test of English as a foreign language. The Japanese rank near the bottom together with Afghanistan, Cambodia and Laos, and recently have fallen behind North Korea.[15]

---

[15] Kathryn Tolbert, "English is the Talk of Japan" in the *Washington Post, 29* January 2000, p. 1.

Some blame for this deficiency must be placed on the system of entrance examinations for high school and college. The written exams focus on fine points of written English grammar and fail to take into account students' ability to speak and understand spoken English. The Japanese government commits up to half a billion dollars a year to run a nation-wide JET program that brings over 5,000 foreign teachers from North America and other English-speaking nations to teach in primary and secondary schools. Sadly, these JET teachers are vastly under-utilized because head English teachers, whose own abilities in English are often shockingly poor, wish to focus on preparing the students for upcoming university entrance exams.

There is a false stereotype that Japanese are very poor language learners. A critical problem is that students do not begin studying English until 7th grade. You could take the same number of average American students, have them take the same number of Japanese classes each week at that age, and the results would be much the same. If current experiments at teaching English to young primary school students are spread nationwide, the chances are that more young Japanese will be inspired to learn more English earlier.

A final problem is Japan's egalitarian approach to learning English. What is needed is some degree of diversity in the education system so that those who really wish to learn English have ample opportunities to study it.

It is better to focus on those who are more talented and truly wish to learn instead of trying on a more universal and egalitarian approach.

JAPANESE FEMALE STUDENTS ARE HIGHLY CRITICAL OF THEIR EDUCATIONAL SYSTEM

While many American educators drool over the supposed excellence of the Japanese educational system and wish they could apply some aspects of Japanese education in their classes, my female students in Japan strongly condemn their system because, they say, it shuns creativity, ignores individuality, and forces them to memorize endless facts which they promptly forget after each exam.

I asked the forty students in my interactive reading class to write a lengthy essay for their midterm project giving their assessments of the strengths and weaknesses of the Japanese educational system. Their responses were almost uniformly negative.

Many of the students cited similar strengths of the Japanese system of education. It does a good job in fostering a sense of discipline, hard work and cooperation. They learn how to work well in groups and how to develop and finish team projects together. They also avoid the selfish pre-occupations of single people in such individually based societies such as the United States.

Virtually all of the students noted, however, that being forced always to seek consensus within a group is not healthy either for them as individuals or for Japan as a nation. Creativity is a very important learning tool if a person wants to achieve the maximum potential in his or her life. One student wrote:

Japanese schools try to get rid of the differences in children, even when the differences are healthy and creative…Japanese educators like uniformity, so it is difficult for students to develop their own personalities and imaginations…J schools must cultivate students' ability of thinking…. They say that one advantage of the system in Japan is that students learn the social skill of cooperation, working together, but it's not true….How can we develop social skills of cooperation if we don't know ourselves as individuals….

Another student added:

How can we develop into full mature adults if we don't learn to make our own decisions without somebody telling us what to do? I wish that we had more opportunities to spread our imagination. We each have our own personalities…If everybody has the same idea, life is not interesting…It is important for us to use our imaginations and to express ourselves.

A foreign teacher in Japan quickly notices that his Japanese students are very afraid to ask questions in class and to respond to questions posed by the instructor. There is a great fear that they will make mistakes and that they will be embarrassed in front of their peers. But, as one student noted, this fear of making errors prevents them from writing to express themselves freely:

Japanese students should have more of a chance to study things that really interest them…Adults destroy most of the intellectual and creative abilities of the students when they push uniformity. We are afraid to make mistakes, take chances, and to follow our true dreams in life…. How can we make creative dreams for our lives? A democratic society needs people who can make choices!

Another added: "Unless we change the educational system, we can never become a creative nation! How can we develop social skills of cooperation if we don't know ourselves as individuals…"

Several students commented that when they are working in a group, nobody learns to take individual responsibility for making bad decisions or even errors. Many of the students wrote that so much time spent studying and cramming for tests and entrance exams robbed them of the chance to have normal childhoods. One student from Aichi Prefecture remembered growing up in a small rural village with only a few students in the whole school. She felt that she was lucky to be close enough to nature to swim in the river and play in the fields. She felt sorry for city children who had to spend all their time cramming in schools.

The students insisted that it is important to have time away from school where they could relax, make good friends, and just enjoy life. One writer recalled that she never spent much time with her family and that nobody ever talked to each other. She added: "Can young people subjected to this void find happiness as adults? We need more time together with family or friends. We need more time to smile and cry together." Another noted sarcastically, "I think students had better study at their own pace and not study too much. As the proverb says, 'All work and no play makes Jack a dull boy!!'"

The students uniformly criticized their Japanese teachers and classes as being repetitive and just plain boring. They noted that it was horribly dull just to sit in class, take notes, stare out the window, constantly look at their watches, and often fall asleep without the teacher noticing or caring because the classes themselves were just huge, often containing as many as forty students. One writer noted that the only classes in which she could express her opinions were English classes, but that her lack of ability in English made it embarrassing to express herself often. Other students complained bitterly about a professor who, rather than giving lectures himself, had students deliver individual reports as the only assigned work in the class. One student said, "We came to this famous university to learn from our professors, not from other students!" I remember passing the open window of one class where perhaps twenty or thirty students were seated aimlessly at the back of a large classroom totally ignoring some somnolent male professor who was reading a lecture that nobody was listening to. It seemed a tragic waste of everybody's time.

Some students stated that Japanese schools are falling behind in terms of modern technology. "We are taught very little about computers and many schools and classes have few if any computers that we can use." Indeed, as many as half of my students said that they have no real idea how to use a computer or word processor.

Some professors go a long way to bring creativity, imagination, and critical thinking into their classes, but their students have already had at least 12 years of a school system that dulled and fatigued their brains beyond belief. The Japanese government would do well to listen to the suggestions of its younger citizens. The nation's successful entry into the 21st century depends on it.

THE DIFFICULT LIVES OF JAPANESE PROFESSORS

The problems facing higher education in Japan are severely compounded by the difficult lives of Japan's college and university professors. Many colleagues at KWC were in general a highly dedicated group of teachers, but their lives were so bogged down by administrative trivia that they had very little time to really prepare for classes and do any of their own research if they were so inclined.

Unlike American universities that generally have strong administrations that share academic power with the faculty, the faculties of Japanese universities wield tremendous collective power while such people as university presidents and deans are generally figureheads with no real function or clout.

University politics faithfully reflect Japan's political culture. Power lies in the hands of powerful factions who govern through consensus and compromise. Tough decisions come only after very lengthy discussions, and if consensus and compromise are not attainable, nothing gets decided. True leaders often remain in the background wielding power like a puppet master who pulls strings behind the stage. Those holding formal reins of leadership may greet guests, sign contracts, and represent the company at functions, but they have no real power to make decisions.

The president and dean of my Kyoto college are full-time members of the faculty who are elected to those posts for short terms. They can be re-elected after two or three years, but if they choose not to run again or are defeated, they return to their old faculty position. They also continue to teach several classes while they serve in office. American college presidents and deans are far too busy generally to teach even one course, but the president and dean of KWC had a heavy load of courses.

Because power is so diffused throughout the college, those seeking power build up support through factions. This feature can be extremely divisive, setting faction against faction, individual against individual. A great amount of time is wasted trying to build factions and striving to achieve consensus or compromise on any one issue or leader.

Meetings are endless and often infringe on precious free time that no American academic would ever give up. Frequently, meetings last late into the night and continue on week-ends; and some professors are obliged to surrender several weeks of their summer break to compose the next year's college entrance exam. My colleagues were perpetually exhausted, so much so that their entire psyche seemed bent out of shape. When my son David visited me in Kyoto, he correctly named Japan the "Land of the Tired." One really wonders how the professors have time to teach effectively and energetically when they are so tired and have so little time to prepare for their classes. It is no small wonder why the already exhausted students complain so bitterly how uninspiring their classes are.

Salaries are very high by American standards—well over $100,000 for a full professor in his or her late forties and early fifties if one adds in the winter and summer bonuses. But life in Japan is also very expensive if you want to live the middle-class dream and many of the professors take second jobs teaching English classes or other tutorials during the evenings and on weekends. KWC generously gives its full-time faculty one day off during the week to pursue their research, but many faculty use that day to teach 2-4 classes as an adjunct at another university. If one includes the six or seven courses (each meets for 90-minutes once a week) they teach at KWC and the three or four they teach on their off day elsewhere, they teach a total of 9-11 classes. I found teaching nine periods a week to be a mind numbing and fatiguing experience and I only did it for one year. It is the definitive example of quantity over quality.

Efforts at open research are all too often stymied by a very restrictive attitude toward who can publish what in whose journals. I ran up against problems when I sent out copies of an article that I had published on the new national government coalition based on research and interviews I had conducted earlier in Tokyo. The article had been quickly snapped up by a leading American periodical, *Asian Survey,* but was rejected by the in-house

Journal for KWC because I was only a temporary employee. I sent the same article to the editor of a journal that dealt with social and political issues at the main university. The article was returned with the simple statement that the

Journal only published articles by members of the university faculty and that even work by professors in other university-affiliated schools was not welcome.

A few older university faculty have published their research in scholarly books that can be purchased anywhere in Japan, and I am told that much of this research and writing is excellent, but much of the faculty's research is limited to in-house publications that are read almost entirely by other colleagues at the school and are not distributed to other colleges and libraries. One wonders how a professor's research and ideas are effectively disseminated to the general academic community if journals published on one campus rarely see the light of day elsewhere.

The difficult and often non-fulfilling life of Japanese academics made the return to my normal American academic life a genuine treat. There was time to prepare for classes, meet my students, rest, and even work on this book.

A LONG AWAITED REFORM

Mombusho officials are finally beginning to think of some possible reforms for the ailing Japanese school system. Starting in 2002, rather than piling on more work for its country's belabored students, Japan will let its young take a rest. Japanese educators want to give students more time to rest, play, to read on their own and to choose more electives that suit their own interests and career goals. Youngsters will be encouraged to develop increased individual initiative. The Mombusho will urge increased creative thinking and individual problem solving at all levels of Japanese education.[16]

Some universities are also commencing reforms that may bring them in line with the changing needs of younger

Japanese. Hosei University near Tokyo, for example, has opened four new undergraduate faculties. The first is an

International Communications Faculty which trains students in the study of foreign languages and cultures and requires all students to spend half of their sophomore year at a foreign university. This approach is especially important for Japanese men, who unlike Japanese women, almost never study abroad and who thus graduate from college woefully ignorant of the world outside Japan.

The next faculty created at Hosei was a Computer Science–Information Services school to train young Japanese in a field still largely ignored by other mainstream Japanese universities. Hosei's novel Humanity and Environment Faculty trains environmental specialists in a vital field often ignored by other schools. The Social Policy and Administration Faculty is designed to produce welfare specialists for a nation which must cope with the difficulties of fewer and fewer children and many more older people.[17] Hosei has opened an extension office in the Silicon Valley in California to provide students and researchers with access to the most sophisticated training in high tech in the world. A program in Entrepreneur education will train students how to open new businesses and in such important areas as individual problem solving.

Students seem to be responding positively to the innovative programs at Hosei University. While 11 of Japan's top private universities each accepted over 40,000 applicants for entrance exams in 2001, Hosei was

---

[16] French, *op. cit.*

[17] Kiyonari Tadao, p. 19.

the only one that had more applicants than in 1992. The major reason for this growth is the fact that it provides younger Japanese as well as mid-career businessmen and women with an opportunity to study in fields directly relevant to the changing needs of Japanese society.

Conclusions

Japanese students thrive and quickly adjust to classroom situations where a focus is placed on the students' active participation in class and he expression and development of their own opinions. Following the example set by Hosei University, the universities must shift their focus towards greater creativity and choice and try to nurture something new: entrepreneurs and independent thinkers.

What is missing in education is the student's sense of personal involvement. There is great student anger at a system that forces them to sit through many very boring courses where the teacher demonstrates a complete lack of concern for their existence. If the teacher would involve the students more in the classes and teach in a more interesting manner, students would gain far more.

The idea that students need to take up to 15-16 courses at once is ludicrous. Very little studying or even learning is going on in these classes and, especially in the case of foreign languages, many are a waste of time.

There must also be a fundamental reform of the entrance exam system. Japanese education is a monumental testimony to the fact that an educational system that bases its success on a series of standardized tests cannot train the youngster to think independently or do well in the real world. Japanese students' lack of success in English is firm testimony of this failure.

Hopefully other Japanese universities will adopt Hosei University's new faculty structure that emphasizes high tech, globalism, and problem solving.

Section II

National Issues And Student Attitudes

One of the goals of this year-long teaching experience in Japan was to learn about the worldview of young Japanese women. I was particularly interested in their attitudes towards careers, marriage, and their own futures. I also sought to discern their views on a variety of issues including politics and such socio-political issues as divorce, the death penalty, the role of gays in society, ethnicity, religion, and what they knew and thought about issues pertaining to war and peace. Such related matters as Japan's handy-phone culture and the unique meaning of Valentine's Day in Japan are also studied as are foreign students in Japan and young geisha.

The following section analyzes the views of female students at KWC on a variety of social and political issues.

I. MODERN JAPANESE WOMEN STILL FACE INTENSE JOB DISCRIMINATION

Recently *New York Times* reporter Howard French commenced a story with the headline, "Diploma in Hand, Japanese Find Glass Ceiling Reinforced with Iron."[18] French correctly notes that throughout the modern era, Japanese companies have utilized a two-tier hiring system. Highly able well-trained men are put on a fast-track that leads eventually to high administrative or even executive positions. Women, however well they have been trained, are placed on a decidedly secondary track. For decades, major companies have operated under the assumption that the proper track for a woman was to work as a secretary for a few years, but then to get married and have children by her mid-twenties, leaving career-building to her husband.

French reports how Yoko Hayakawa, a senior at Keio, one of Japan's elite universities in Tokyo, discovered a pattern that struck her as being very strange when she went for a round of interviews with technology companies in Tokyo recently:

Although she had been getting excellent grades, spoke English fluently, and was bursting with professional ambition, all the recruiters were asking trivial questions about her social life or how she would feel about accepting a clerical position. 'One company asked if I would work as a secretary, instead of in a technical job. Another company asked if I was going to see a concert that was being held near my campus. One recruiter even asked me how many convenience stores there were in Japan. When I asked around among my male friends, they had not heard any questions like

---

[18] Howard W. French, "Diploma in Hand, Japanese Women Find Glass Ceiling Reinforced with Iron" in the *New York Times,* January 1, 2001, p. 1.

these at all. They were asked the normal sorts of things, like what they had studied at school, and what their ambitions were if they were hired.[19]

French concludes that her experience is very representative of the intense discrimination women face at the work place in Japan.

Most of my students in Kyoto began their grueling job search process late in their junior year. They visited job fairs and recruiting agencies and made the rounds to various companies, all hoping to find a worthy job that would begin a year later, on April 1st , roughly two weeks after their graduation.

The job search made a mockery of my students' senior year because they were always on the road seeking interviews. One of my seniors was a delightfully bright young woman who spoke fluent English because she had grown up in California. She came to class only 12 of the 27 times the class met and submitted fewer than half of her assigned essays. Her excuse was that she was always searching in vain for a job, but I wanted to flunk her because juniors in the class were doing all the work while she did so little. But flunking her would have meant that she would not have graduated and her advisor, a senior Japanese professor, strongly urged me to pass her. She did pass with a grade of 60. I was very upset that this student would get credit for a course that she deserved to flunk, but that is how life is conducted in Japan where true academic standards seem to count for little, at least for women.

Students who have studied for a year or more in the United States, Australia, Canada or Britain usually do much better than those who lack international experience and skills in English or other foreign languages. The very lucky ones get hired by foreign companies with branches in Japan. They are often treated with far more respect and dignity than they would encounter in a typical Japanese company. Foreign firms very often promote women to positions of influence and power.

---

19 Ibid.

However, foreign-trained Japanese women can do well with Japanese companies, especially if they are small, newish firms that are not laced with eons of tradition and older male Japanese executives whose attitudes towards women can be very discriminatory indeed. A considerable number of my foreign-trained (and even some who had developed excellent English skills on their own) got acceptable posts with smaller hi-tech firms in the Kyoto-Osaka area. Most of the same women, however, report that when they approached larger corporations, interviewers wanted to shunt them off into secretarial track or other dead-end jobs.

It is ironic that the population of younger Japanese, those in their twenties and thirties, will shrink by a third by 2015. This is indeed worrisome, because such a shrinkage in the youthful workforce will have obvious detrimental effects on the economy. Clearly, part of the problem could be met by hiring more women into responsible positions.

The Japanese government enacted a new equal opportunity law in 2000 which for the first time mandates punishments for discriminating against women in the work place. But thus far it seems that the law has had little effect because at least in Japan, it is very hard to actually legislate new ways of social behavior.

The major rationale used by companies for excluding women from professional jobs is the fear that they will quit to get married only a few years after their employment. Companies invest considerable amounts of time and money in training their permanent workers, and an employee who leaves shortly after the training can represent a significant loss. Companies, especially in periods of recession, know that there are higher risks hiring women employees and they do not want to risk losing their investment in human capital.

Other surveys, however, show that a cast majority of women would like to remain in the work force until retirement age. Some women find that they must quit their jobs when they have children due to the high cost of day care. If such care were both more available and less costly, more women could keep their day jobs. While some companies do have maternity leave policies, they often find somebody else sitting at their desks when they return and that their career momentum has been muted.

Japanese have also long opposed significant immigration to help handle labor shortages, but because of the population time bomb that threatens to devastate the country, some companies and government officials appear willing to make compromises to bring in more foreigners rather than hire their own women.

One of my former Japanese students, who graduated from KWC's Junior College in the early 1990s and from Mary Baldwin College with an honors degree in International Relations two years later, has had a hard time "making it" despite fluency in English and strong experience abroad. She worked briefly in Kobe as a secretary for a small import-export company which "down-sized" her and other staff just days before the company itself was destroyed in the 1995 earthquake. She quickly moved to a trading company in Osaka where she had a decent salary and important responsibilities, but she quit three years later to try her luck with the Tokyo branch of an American company. She was hired as the secretary to the Japanese president of the Tokyo office, but chafed at her generally clerical duties that could have been performed just as well by a high school graduate.

The Japanese male managers treated her badly, but she befriended an American manager on loan from the Texas headquarters, who quickly recognized her talents and got her promoted to an administrative position in sales over the strong objections of the Japanese male hierarchy. But despite her triumphant success, she grew increasingly tired of the daily stress and lack of creativity in her job. She hoped to get married in 2001 to her boyfriend, who has a good job with a more traditional Japanese firm. Unlike his fiancée, however, he had graduated from a Japanese university, had never been abroad, had never even flown in an airplane, and she always complained that he was insensitive to her career aspirations because she is female.

II. JAPANESE WOMEN, AMERICAN DREAMS

A surprising number of my female university students in Kyoto expressed a desire, however whimsical, to emigrate from Japan to the United States with a clear desire to live out the American dream of achieving wealth and independence. Even though many of these students come from wealthy families who can afford to send them to one of the most prestigious colleges in Japan, they openly complained about living in a country that fails to provide them with any chance of either a meaningful career or true independence. These young, well-educated women feel that they are trying to escape the realities of their homeland. They stress that Japan fails to offer them enough in the way of opportunity because they are women.

Their point is well taken. Even though many female graduates are better educated and far more worldly than their Japanese male counterparts, they face a male-dominated government and business establishment that remains quite hostile to the genuine advancement of women. For every one woman who does achieve wealth and/or independence on her own, most others fail. One student noted: "We are not treated equally here and we never will be. We want to free ourselves from everything. Our only alternative is to escape to the US where all women do have equality." Even if such statements are made more out of frustration than any real desire to leave their homeland, it does indicate that some younger, better educated Japanese women long for greener pastures.

A small, but growing minority is trying to realize thisAmerican dream. Some enroll for a time in American colleges and universities while many more diligently study English hard at colleges like KWC. A growing but still small handful try to move to the US each year, but most fail and quietly return because they lack the basic practical skills and background to make it in America.[20]

One can sense a growing degree of anger and frustration among female college students in Japan. Over 60% of my 200 students fear that they will be trapped in a loveless marriage with a workaholic husband who will pay little heed to his family. A quarter of my students declare that not marrying is the best way to a life of freedom and independence and that they will either stay single or else marry a foreigner who will treat them well.

Ironically, it appears that women themselves rather than the male establishment have been the major barrier to progress in the area of women's rights. Men do create barriers, but at least a few ambitious women do indeed "make it." So many Japanese women have such low confidence in their own ability and chances for success that they defeat themselves. Japanese women need to liberate themselves and change their way of thinking—rather than thinking of escaping to the US.

One of my brightest, most attractive and best English-speaking students, Eri Tsuchiya, told me in class that after graduation she hoped to become a hotel receptionist or ground hostess for an airline where she might be able to use her English. She was stunned when I told her that a woman with her ability and intelligence should aim much higher than the servile positions she was considering.

For her it was a question of confidence. Even though she had spent a whole year studying English at a small American college in Tennessee and was one of my most adept and hardworking students, she felt overwhelmed by the barriers placed against women in Japan. But after taking classes with foreign teachers and students at KWC, she seemed to experience considerable changes in her perspectives on life.[21]

---

[20] The American dream sentiment is expressed in the following letter I received in late 2000 from a former student at KWC who found a surprisingly good office job after graduation.

"After graduation I will start working. I don't know how long I will continue the job, but I will do my best. But some day, I will stop; working, and want to go to the US. I don't know [whether I should]…work ? Study? But I really really want to go to the US because there I can do what I want and rise in my career. Now I am studying for obtaining a license of an interpreter or a translator.

[21] Eighteen months later the same student, now a second-semester senior at KWC, wrote me to tell of her new job:

Japan has never had a viable feminist movement because most Japanese women have never developed a feminist worldview. It is indeed interesting to note that since the Meiji era those few women who have "made it" professionally were often pushed hard and promoted by their fathers. Japanese women will never make much progress until they alter their perceptions of themselves and see that doors will open if they have the courage and tenacity to open them.

III. RACISM AND ETHNICITY IN JAPAN

A jewelry store owner in the city of Hamamatsu (Shizuoka) paid the price in 1999 for racist behavior when a court there ordered him to pay more than $US 15,000. The

Court determined that he had ordered a Brazilian out of his store simply because she was a forcigner. The case developed when Ana Bortz, a Brazilian journalist living in Hamamatsu, walked into the jewelry store in June 1998. While she was looking at some jewelry on display, the shop owner approached her and asked her nationality. When Bortz replied that she was Brazilian, the owner told her that foreigners were banned from the store. He tried to force Bortz out, showing her a police pamphlet warning

---

I found a new job for the next year after graduation. I will stay in Kyoto where I will work at a small company which develops an sells instruments for natural science research. All this is very new to me, but it looks interesting. The company only has two employees now, but next spring 2 fellow students will join them. The boss needs people who can speak English, so we were hired. I will do all sorts of things in the job including accounting, public relations, management. They also advertise their products at conferences held at universities, so I will also travel. I was very interested in the diversity of my work here…It should be interesting.

But I will continue studying English with the hope of finding a job some day that I really want. But I still don't know what I want to do. There are so many things I want to do. Now what I am thinking is to be an interpreter, Japanese teacher, or something like that.

against theft. The store owner had also set up signs in his store declaring foreigners to be banned from the premises.

Bortz sued after the owner refused to issue a written apology. The owner told the court he had to limit the number of customers entering the store as a crime-prevention measure. The judge told the court: "Banning foreigners from a store has an element of treating them cruelly because of their differences and is not appropriate

Behavior…. The nation is a signatory to the International Convention on the Elimination of All Forms of Racial Discrimination and that treaty is as effective as domestic law."

This kind of incident occurs fairly often in Japan, especially to non-European foreigners. An English writer noted recently: "Although they regard themselves as superior to all other peoples, the Japanese are generally friendly and kind to foreign visitors. As for foreigners of European extraction, they are generally given far better treatment than are fellow Japanese; non-Japanese Asians or those of non-white races, such as Africans, may not receive a fraction of such overwhelmingly good treatment…. A disturbing occurrence in recent years has been the release of large numbers of anti-Semitic books, this despite the presence of only a tiny number of Jews in the country, all of them foreigners."

The writer notes that while temporary foreign guests receive extraordinarily warm treatment, this attitude changes greatly when the guest takes up longer residence. The warm guest treatment turns to a neutral stance. He quickly observes a we vs. they attitude of Japanese who want these foreign guests to serve as useful tools, but who don't want them to stay beyond their period of maximum usefulness. He correctly notes that the chief value of a prolonged working stay in Japan is self-discovery and self-realization.

Although racism in Japan is far more muted than in places like the United States or Britain, it does indeed exist. Japan has a very homogeneous population and is quite ethnocentric. Japan will resort to almost any measure to insure ethnic purity, and while many foreigners continue to reside in Japan, they are considered guests who must be tolerated at best. When I interviewed several Japanese Dietmen and government officials about Japan's inevitable population decline, I suggested the alternative of immigration to bring in young workers. All those interviewed rejected the possibility, urging instead plans or measures to increase the supply of purely Japanese babies.

Any foreigner can experience stares and snubs fairly often. A food store owner giving out free samples with-draws her plate as I approach. A drunken old man hits me on the head with a newspaper on a train and tells me—"Foreigner **GO** Home!" While commuting to work, on occasion I heard the same message from young Japanese men aboard the Kintetsu train. Other students and foreign friends who have lived here for a while say much the same thing.

Most Japanese treat me and other foreigners very well indeed, but one is always reminded that there is a very clear line between Japanese and non-Japanese and that it is virtually impossible for a foreigner to become a Japanese citizen. Japan is also a very parochial place with only the thinnest of international concerns and outlooks.

Unlike the Philippines which supports many different cultural groups, Japan is the antithesis of a melting pot.

Indeed, there are increasing contacts between Japan and the outside world as many Japanese, particularly young women, travel and study abroad. Japanese who have lived abroad have a far more tolerant intercultural outlook. But a rising sense of cultural nationalism among some Japanese continues to darken the waters.

ETHNICITY IN JAPAN:

Another furor concerns hot spring bath resorts in Otaru, Hokkaido that have decided to ban all foreigners; apparently *gaijin* are too noisy and smell bad and most Japanese customers would rather stay away than share the baths with gaijin. A related controversy concerns a serious Western scholar who recently published a book showing the very diverse ethnic origins of the Japanese people. The book is denounced by some Japanese scholars who proclaim a primordialist view of ethnicity, the notion that the Japanese Volk was created from a single pure line.

Ethnic purity means a lot to Japanese and creates a gap between Japanese and non-Japanese. You must be born Japanese to be Japanese and, as is especially the case for many Koreans, even if your family has lived in Japan for many generations, you cannot become Japanese. Reviewer Donald Richie notes: "The idea that culture and 'ethnos' are closed, bounded units, that there is an essential Japanese psychic unity that permeates these various cultural building blocks—these are perhaps anachronistic ideals, but they persist....It is accepted by many people in contemporary Japan that only ethnic Japanese can speak Japanese fluently; foreigners who become highly proficient in the language are usually seen as somehow threatening exceptions to the rule....There is a similar widespread assumption that people who do not look Japanese cannot be Japanese citizens."

One of my students in Kyoto wrote an essay lamenting that although her Korean family (from the northern part of Korea) has lived in Japan for over 100 years, few Japanese would marry her and she must get a North Korean passport if she ever hopes to travel abroad (Its like saying that since my German great-grandfather migrated from Germany in the 1880s, I cannot be American and must apply for a German passport). She has no civil rights and cannot meet her greatest wish, a chance to study in the US, because it is impossible for her to get a North Korean passport.

One may call this ethnic nationalism or simple racism, but it is a very big fact of life here. Even otherwise liberal professors at KWC would not support immigration to handle Japan's emerging population crisis and only 30% of Japanese would even consider marrying a foreigner.

PESSIMISM, ANTI-FOREIGN FEELINGS AND LACK OF INTEREST IN TECHNOLOGY MAY HURT JAPAN

During my year in Kyoto in Japan I sensed that the worldview of the Japanese has changed considerably from the views held by Japanese when I was here in the 1960s, 1970s, 1980s, and very early 1990s. Japan's prolonged economic recession seems to have brought on an intense sense of pessimism, isolationism and anger towards the outside world. A recent study by the Dentsu Institute clearly supports these views.

The sense of pessimism runs very deep. Only 36.6 percent of Japanese responded positively to a question asking if they think that Japan will be better off in the next ten years—-this figure is very low when compared to positivist Koreans (91.4%) and Chinese (87.9). Only Berliners (37.5%) shared Japan's dour outlook.

The reasons for Japanese pessimism are readily apparent. When asked what aspects of their country excel in comparison to others, only 'safety' topped 50%. Despite having the world's 2nd largest economy, only 17.8% of Japanese said that they could be proud of their economic power. Sadly, only 1.8% said 'international leadership7; still less, 1.7% said "international political power." Only 29.4% applauded the "quality of the people.

Japan's growing isolation and antipathy for foreigners is evident. To put it simply, in an age of growing globalization, Japan is becoming greatly hostile to anything and anyone foreign. According to the survey, 76.9% of Japanese say that they cannot speak any English at all. 48.6 of Japanese said that they had no interest in news or information about the outside world. Only a third said that they had any tolerance for international marriages involving Japanese.

A recent article in the daily Mainichi reflected these trends. Several websites based in Japan had been set up to encourage improved rights and living conditions for foreigners in Japan and to encourage support for the rights of World War II era comfort women. The sites were inundated with so many ugly, racist and anti-foreign statements that they were forced to shut down.

Any student of Japanese history will tell you that Japan historically goes through sharply different phases of opening itself to the outside world (cosmopolitan) and being very closed (isolationist). The Japanese were closed during the Edo period (1600s-1860s), very open during the Meiji period (roughly 1860s to about 1905), closed from about 1905 through the end of World War II, very open after World War II to the early 1990s, and then closed starting in the late 1990s.

The tragedy is that Japan cannot afford isolationism at a time of growing internationalism. But the increased racism, isolationism, and hostility do not make Japan a pleasant place for many foreigners to reside.

IV. A QUESTION OF SELF-IDENTITY

One of the favorite questions both Japanese and foreign journalists like asking about the current young generation is whether these people have an identity that is distinctly Japanese. Actress Youki Kudoh in a 1999 *Time* essay "Who Killed our Culture? We Did" writes that while her grandparents' generation endured hunger and poverty after World War II, they and their children showered their anger and frustration at the state which had brought so much pain to them—so much so that they even refused to sing the national anthem. "The result was that we of the younger generation were taught that patriotism is bad. If you express your love for your country, you are called 'pro-war,' you are considered a right-winger."[22]

Kudoh notes that younger Japanese have grown up and prospered under the shadow of American economic and pop culture (Coke, music, dance, family life etc.).

---

[22] Youki Kudoh, "Who Killed Our Culture? We Did" in *Time* (Asia), 3-10 May, 1999, p. 50

Most of today's young people grew up in the absence of some important values. They aren't positive about being Japanese, nor about their own identity. They are losing their integrity because they always pretend to be like someone else. Whatever becomes popular, they want to follow. When girls put on platform shoes that are popular now, it is as if they are trying to step up to another level, to become someone they are not. These girls want long legs, big breasts and Caucasian features. The sense of beauty has changed. Young women don't recognize what is good about themselves.

We have become polluted by American culture, contaminated by materialism. We don't love our country, don't respect it… We are negative about our culture; traditional things are seen as old-fashioned, and everything new is good. Social order and moral standards have disappeared. Some people are even obsessed with denying their Japaneseness. Many girls dye their hair and tan their skin. The streets and towns of Japan are made to look like France or America….Traditional culture is not even accessible to most of us; it is disappearing into oblivion.

Usually we compromise too much of ourselves. What is missing in young people, I think, is the ability to establish a relationship with a person without trying to copy that person, or comparing whether you are richer or poorer, or better or worse. We need to love ourselves, take pride in our homeland, and establish fair and equal relationships with people from all over the world. You can accept somebody without losing your identity. We need the confidence with which to see the good qualities hidden in our history and tell the world about them. We need a flexible mind with which we can learn about mistakes in our history and turn them into positive lessons.

I presented Kudoh's essay to my junior-level academic-writing class and asked for their written and oral responses. The result was a very intense discussion and passionate essays. A large minority of the students strongly agreed with Ms. Kudoh and mourned the loss of a distinct sense of being Japanese.

One student noted: "We are a very parochial people and we have lost touch with our past. We have no foundation and spend so much time copying outsiders that we don't know ourselves."

Another wrote: "Japanese are copying Americans too much. They don't have originality. Every place I look, I see girls with the same kind of hairstyles, clothes and jewelry. Kudoh says that Japanese don't respect their own country and culture. We can see that by the fashion styles now popular in Japan...Japanese should respect their culture and their country before bringing in American culture..."

A majority of the students, however, strongly disagreed with Kudoh. One of my best students, Eri Tsuchiya, wrote:

"Japan certainly does have its own identity. We still have traditional culture, food, clothing and a Japanese spirit. Younger Japanese may copy American styles and are very conspicuous on the streets—there is nothing really traditionally Japanese about them. But deep down their behavior is still very Japanese. They eat Japanese food, mainly sleep on futons, don't wear shoes in the house, still respect elders, and in general think like Japanese." Japanese may not be conscious of their patriotism and we often admire American or European cultures...., but when we have the Olympics or world championships in some sports, our people cheer very loudly for Japan. Patriotism is very much here."

Another wrote:

"Being very clever is part of the Japanese way. The Germans may make a new kind of car, but very quickly we Japanese will copy it and make it better. We take Indian curry recipes and rearrange them to fit our tastes. To copy the ideas of others and to adapt them to our way of life is ***INDEED*** the essence of Japanese culture at its best. After all, Japanese culture is not dead. It is original for Japanese to copy and adapt from outside."

I myself find that while Japan is always changing and adapting ideas from the outside, the essential heart of Japanese culture is ever-present in the minds and personalities of my 225 students here—that they are proud of their country, proud to be Japanese, and although many want to live abroad for part of their lives, they will all remain at heart Japanese.

V. REMEMBERING THE WAR: JAPAN'S HISTORIC MYOPIA

Teaching and researching in Japan brought my attention to different and yet very related intellectual phenomena: the vast ignorance and misinformation that Japanese college students have concerning their own history and the attempt by various Japanese scholars to revise the whole framework of Japanese history.

One of the major topics discussed over the past few decades in Japanese academic circles and the press is the debate over the nature of Japan's participation in the Pacific War. There is no question today that Japan as a whole is a thoroughly pacifist nation. There is no military of any consequence and only a few Japanese at the fringe of Japanese politics call for full rearmament. A number of Japanese novelists and poets have produced a meaningful number of anti-war books dating back to the late 1940s and in recent years a number of private museums have put on displays that do not look favorably on Japan's involvement in the war.

There is indeed an important segment of the Japanese population, perhaps more to the left politically than most Japanese, who want Japanese to see the full dimension of how Japan inflicted so much pain on other Asians as well as to remember how much Japanese themselves suffered. Some school texts published in the 1990s at least take note of the aggressive nature of Imperial Japan during World War II, but most young Japanese today remain blissfully ignorant of the whole World War II era.

The "Peace Museum" at Hiroshima for many years had exhibits that portrayed Japan as the "victim" in the war.

There were endless exhibits of the horrible suffering endured by Japanese as a result of American bombing of the Japanese mainland, but absolutely no mention of the misery the Japanese inflicted on other Asians. Dozens of my American students who viewed those exhibits came out thinking that this one-sided approach was not fair, but more recent exhibits do in fact reaffirm the fact that Japan was both aggressor and victim by at least mentioning how Japan ravaged China, etc.

It is also true that historic revisionism is a hot topic in Japan today. A number of scholars, journalists, and other establishment figures who are quite literally trying to rewrite or at least reframe the traditional view of Japan's involvement in World War II. They are casting Japan's war effort as a very noble cause to free the rest of Asia from the clutches of Western colonial imperialism and suggesting that Japan's war leaders were benign heroes who gave their lives for the good of the nation.

The revisionist scholars decry the more traditional view of Japanese history during World War II—Japan's murderous aggression in China and the rest of Asia, its attack on Pearl Harbor, its dreadful torture of millions of other Asians and its use of sex slavery— as an American image, a form of victor's justice where the winner gets to write its version of the war and to punish the losers in any way they see fit. They prefer to view the war in a more positive light and deny that the uglier truths of the war such as the Rape of Nanjing and the sex slavery ever took place or at the most were great exaggerations of the truth. The revisionists insist that Japanese children will have a horrible image of their country and will be ashamed of being Japanese if all they are taught are the negative lies of the past.

The impact that the revisionists have had on what younger Japanese study about in school is hard to gauge, but my students had a "Japan as the Sufferer" image of the war in which the aggressive West inflicted needlessly intense bombing—including atomic bombing—on a nearly defenseless Japan. Several students expressed anger over what the US did at Hiroshima, but were stunned and puzzled when I told them about the murder of 30-50 million Asians by the Japanese army, the sex-slavery, Unit 731 (which conducted biological "experiments" on living Chinese), the Rape of Nanjing etc.

Every nation has its extreme nationalists and scholars who wish to rewrite history, but what surprises me about Japan is the support the revisionists get from Japan's conservative elite leadership establishment in politics, business, the bureaucracy, and the media. To talk about conspiracies would be absurd, but it does appear that many establishment conservative figures wish to control a Japan that has a more "honored" view of its past.

The conservative establishment that led Japan before 1945 was the big loser in World War II. Occupation forces under General MacArthur wrote a very liberal and democratic constitution and sought to lay the groundwork for a progressive and democratic society where power actually lay in the hands of the people. The lower classes saw the American occupation as their liberation from the claws of the elite who had driven Japan to defeat.

Since World War II, The conservative establishment has been trying to return to its dominant position in society. Its view of Japan differs sharply from that imposed by the Americans—a modified imperial system, a carefully managed society that is much less democratic than today, and a "correct view" of history that whitewashes all of the ugliness of defeat.

Historical revisionism thus seems to be part of a much bigger package. The tragedy is that it appears to be working.... Japanese college students have a very weak understanding of the War era and perceive Japan as a true victim. Younger Japanese have no interest in politics and rarely vote. Hence they seemed surprised when I implored them to vote in local elections and when I offered them my version of World War II history. Indeed, they seem very uncomfortable and a bit upset with the Japan-As-Aggressor motif even when I point out parallels in American history.

One of my students contributed the following essay on the topic:

Japan has a very long history. The history lectures in school focus entirely on dates and facts. Japanese students have few opportunities to study history objectively so as to develop a real under-standing of their history. One of the reasons for this state is our educational system, which harms the student by cramming little bits of knowledge into their heads.

We Japanese students must memorize vast amounts of dates and facts for the college entrance exams, but there is no need to know the circumstances surrounding these facts.

The Japanese government does not disclose the real truth of history. Our texts make no mention of the Rape of Nanking and the Comfort Women. One cannot blame young Japanese for their ignorance and their failure to understand why other Asians mistrust us. Sadly we young Japanese carry the future of our nation on our shoulders, so we must know our true history to be able to have good diplomacy with other nations.

The Japanese government censors every text book and blots out any mention of the cruelty that the Japanese military inflicted on other Asians during the War. The Japanese government cannot hide the tragedies of the past from itself and its children. Japanese leaders should accept responsibility and realize that history tells us who we are. We cannot claim to have a sense of morality if we do not know the reality of Japanese history. Any person can make a mistake, but he is truly guilty if he fails to learn from that mistake and does it all over again.

Koreans and Chinese today have a negative image of Japanese owing to our myopic view of our own history. Just as a person cannot live in total isolation, a country must live in a community of nations. Japan needs to have good relations with its neighbors. We share close ethnic ties with our neighbors, but we cannot become friends until we can come to terms with our past.

As a young Japanese, I must truly understand what our history is about. I must confront it boldly even though it is merciless. One of my friends who is a Korean woman told me that she has a negative image of Japanese. Her parents and grandparents also feel the same. Her comments deeply hurt me and it was only then that I realized how cruel my country's actions had been. Japan cannot have a bright future if it insists on neglecting its past.[23]

JAPAN'S WARTIME AROCITIES AND FAILURE TO APOLOGIZE

An article in the *Japan Times* in October 1999 sent me into a deep rage. It recounted the sad tale of Song Sin Do, a 77-year-old South Korean resident of Japan who was a sex slave to the Japanese army during World War II. She had sued the Japanese government demanding financial redress (compensation) for her suffering. The Tokyo District Court summarily dismissed her case on October lst, 1999.

According to her deposition, Song was 16 and living in Japanese-occupied Korea in 1938 when an elderly Korean woman told her that she could earn a better living by working for the country at the front lines where Japanese and Chinese troops were fighting. She was taken to a brothel called "Sekaikan" in Wuchang, a city along the Yangtze River in China, along with fifteen other girls. Later she was taken via military vehicle to several other brothels in different cities. Japanese soldiers came to the brothels from morning til night and she was obliged to let them rape her regardless of her state of health. By the time Japan surrendered, she had been held for seven years. Song demanded about $120,000 and a formal apology.

The Court acknowledged that she had been a sex slave, but rejected her claims, noting that individuals do not have the right to sue the state, that the 20-year statute of limitations ran out long ago, and that the government is not obliged to compensate victims as individuals. The Court also noted that the pre-war Meiji Constitution, which was in effect at the time,

---

[23] Essay by Kanae Shinozaki, a Japanese student now a senior at Mary Baldwin College (December, 2000)

said that the government does not bear responsibility for individual damages inflicted by the government.

The great tragedy is that Ms. Song, now an old and frail woman, will probably die without having her honor restored through an apology. To put it simply, the Japanese government through its soldiers authorized her capture and repeated rape for many years and now it does not have the decency to say, "We did something horrible and we apologize." To dismiss her case on technical grounds and to ignore Ms. Song's human pain is in effect raping her again.

Mature, honorable people often make horrible mistakes, but when they see the impact of their folly, they at the very least offer a sincere apology and may even offer restitution. Dishonorable people who run from their crimes, who fail to acknowledge their guilt, are not worthy of membership in civilized society.

Japan has a hard time acknowledging its past wrongs. An accompanying article in the *Japan Times* describes a new book by two prominent history professors while claims that the 1936 Nanking massacre in China never occurred—that it was a "forgery of history" concocted by the victors of World War II to tarnish the image of Japan for their own political and economic benefit. In addition, the writers agree that the best selling book, *The Rape of Nanking* by Iris Chang, is in fact not a book written by a single writer, but a systematically anti-Japanese campaign by pro-Chinese forces in the US. One of the authors, Shudo Higashinakano, claimed that Chang's book will only bring unfortunate repercussions for future Japanese-Chinese relations, adding that such an anti-Japanese campaign typified by Chang's book is only one segment of what he calls "today's information war" and he urged Japanese people to "appropriately appreciate" the nation's history to protect national interests. Sadly, many high placed individuals in Japan's conservative government support these claims.

Most nations in Asia cannot press Japan on the sex slave issue because they depend on Japanese economic ties and investment for their own economic survival. There seems to be an unwritten agreement that they will all avoid discussing the claims by the surviving "comfort women" until they conveniently all die in the near future.

Nevertheless, the publication of Japanese textbooks that support a revisionist view of history can and often does poison relations between Japan and its neighbors like North and South Korea and China. There was an explosion of anger in these countries in early 2001 when the Japanese Ministry of Education approved a new text, *The Junior High School Social Studies New History Textbook,* by two revisionist Japanese historians, Tadae Takubo and Nobukatsu Fujioka.

Takubo and Fujioka say that they wrote the revisionist text because there is "too little patriotism" in contemporary Japan. They want to present an alternative view of history to that "fabricated by the victors" in which Japan "was made to bear sole responsibility for the ravages of war." Their revised text is necessary, they claim, because a defeated Japan had never been permitted to present its case to its own citizens.[24]

The authors argue that claims of Japanese atrocities in the war are "wartime propaganda...just a rumor," that descriptions of Japan's cruel occupations of other Asian states are one-sided, and that the "Greater East Asian War" was really a battle to secure independence for Asian peoples from their Western oppressors. These revisionists add that Allied histories forget to mention the roads, bridges, and other infrastructure built in Korea by the Japanese that brought Korea into the modern world. Angry Koreans rebut this claim by recalling a brutal occupation of their country in which hundreds of thousands of men were forced into virtual slavery, two hundred thousand women were kidnapped for sexual services as "comfort women" and Japanese occupation authorities tried to stamp out the use of the Korean language and Korean names.

---

[24] Doug Struck, "New Text Reopening Old Wounds: Revisionist History in Japan Minimizes Atrocities Before, During WWII" in *The Washington Post,* 18 April 2001.

Critics of the new text, both in Japan and elsewhere in Asia, argue that millions of young Japanese will grow up with a perverted view of Japanese history and little understanding why so many other Asians hate and distrust Japan. At the same time, these critics of revisionist history suggest that other Asians will distrust a Japan that refuses to confront its past and that the many controversies relating to the War will not fade until Japan can honestly come to terms with its past.

Japanologist Mark A. Riddle, participating in a Japan Forum discussion on anti-American feeling in Japan in 2001, responds to the statement, "Japan's resurgent nationalism is thoroughly anti-American."[25]

Were I asked to formally defend this proposition, I would offer as Exhibit A a book published just last month (May 20) and already a best-seller: 'Daiyon no Kokunan' [Fourth National Crisis] by Maeno Tooru.

It's all here: Japan was lured into WWII by Roosevelt; the East Asia war was for Japan both a war of self-defense and a crusade to liberate Asia from Western racism and colonialism; Truman was a war criminal equal to Hitler; the Tokyo War Crimes Trials were a violation of international law, etc. The book's title refers to its argument that Japan's current "dependence" on America is a national crisis equal to the Mongol invasion of the 13th C, the Tokugawa-Meiji (1854-68) transition and the defeat of 1945.

This book should resolve the debate about whether or not Ishihara Shintaro is really anti-American: he wrote its preface, "This is the book I wanted to write." But this book is very important for another reason: it's a declaration of Japanese nationalism's new "historical narrative." Nations, like individuals, have destinies which are predictable because they are based on self-concepts which become self-fulfilling prophecies. Japan's

---

[25] Mark Riddle, Japan Forum, 15 June 2001 (japanforum@lists.nbr.org)

nationalists see themselves as victims of the US bully; the U.S. and a Japan with a resurgent nationalism are on a collision course.

Coming to terms with the past also means having an objective understanding of history. The ignorance my students have of modern Japanese history is both shameful and astounding. When one of my brightest students openly asserted in class that the Nanking Massacre was a fabrication, that it had never occurred, she reflected the opinions of the other students as well. When they have no idea who Kita Ikki or Admiral Yamamoto or General Tojo were, or why Japan invaded China or attacked Pearl Harbor, they become ready victims for the right-wing propagandists whose text books are being approved by the Ministry of Education.

I and several American guest speakers had very constructive discussions with these students once we mentioned some of our own nation's less than honorable deeds including the slaughter of innocent Vietnamese civilians during the Vietnam War, the fire bombing of Tokyo in March 1945, the internment of Japanese-Americans during World War II, slavery and our genocide on native Americans. These frank dialogues gave us all a better perspective of our mutual histories and relationships.

JAPANESE SHARE MIXED FEELINGS CONCERNING KOSOVO WAR

The tragedy of Kosovo seemed very far away if your base is in Japan. Although page one of *The New York Times* was full of Kosovo news, there was absolutely no mention of the war at all in this morning's (May 24, 1999) *Kyoto Shimbun*. Last night's NHK (Japan's BBC) mentioned the war briefly near the end of the broadcast after a cutesy piece on animals in China. I never heard the war being discussed among any of my Japanese colleagues.

To get some gauge of Japanese opinion, I lectured on the war in two of my junior-level classes, discussed it further with the students, and handed them recent editorials from the *Times* and *Washington Post*. I assigned the students a 2-3 page essay where they were asked to give their assessment of NATO's bombing campaign.

The responses came in last week. It was amazing how hard the students worked on researching the topic and then writing their essays. They were most excited about the topic because they claimed that they rarely if ever discuss current events topics in class and are rarely asked to express their views on any meaningful topic.

The attitude most clearly revealed by the essays is that there is a very strong pacifist streak among younger Japanese. They have inherited a fear and hatred for war and violence from their parents and grandparents. There was an acknowledgement, however, that the military alliance with the US is very necessary because of China's growing power as well as other threats from North Korea. They noted that a re-armed Japan could stir passions in Korea and China and that American bases in Japan are a necessity that Japan must pay dearly for.

All of the students strongly condemned Serbian butchery of Albanian Crossovers, but they were puzzled over any appropriate response. Roughly half the students condemned the NATO bombing, noting that violence is not a justifiable response to violence—that it just makes the situation worse. These students said that the bombing would accomplish little and was not worth the destruction of detente between the West and Russia and China.

The remaining responses gave guarded support for the NATO bombing campaign. They said that one simply could not stand by and watch the slaughter of so many innocent people and that while the bombing campaign thus far had failed to end ethnic cleansing, it was sending a clear message to Serbia and other states that the slaughter of innocent people could not go unnoticed. A couple of students, however, wondered where the West was when there was so much slaughter in Rwanda 3-4 years ago.

VI. YOUNG WOMEN AND POLITICS: DOES THEIR INDIFFERENCE BODE POORLY FOR DEMOCRACY IN JAPAN?

Early each January Japan celebrates the annual "Coming of Age" day to honor those young Japanese who recently celebrated their twentieth birthdays, thus becoming legal adults. They can now legally drink and vote and carry on the other normal responsibilities of other adult Japanese, but they exhibit increased nihilist attitudes towards public life. They have a strong reputation for not voting, not reading newspapers or following the news, and of being dangerously ignorant of history and the world around them. This "Generation-X" is said to be an alienated group focused mainly on its own needs and caring very little about others.

Several Japanese newspapers sent out reporters to determine what young Japanese feel about politics, public affairs, and politicians in general. Many of these new adults said that they would indeed vote in the next general election held in late spring 2000, but their comments also revealed mixed feelings about politics in general and hostility and distrust towards many politicians. The youths sampled noted that they would vote out of a sense of duty, but displayed little enthusiasm and considerable apathy. Since dozens of my own students celebrated their own adult womanhood that Monday, I asked over 80 students in several of my classes to fill out a questionnaire concerning their general views towards politics in Japan. The results of these surveys strongly reflected trends found in other recent surveys.

The results of my survey of 80 19-20-yr.-old women are as follows:

YES   NO   UNSURE

Will you vote in the 2000 election?

65   30   5

Are you at all interested in politics?

30   60   10

Do you trust Japan's political leaders?

10   80   10

Detail—Question 1: Those who say that they intend to vote generally see it as their responsibility or civic duty even though they won't vote with much enthusiasm. The general feeling was that, "I have acquired the right and thus should use it," but there were exceptions to this apathy. One student wrote, "Voting is our responsibility. Many people have fought and died for this right." Other comments included: "We have no right to criticize politicians unless we vote." "Even one vote can change the fate of Japan."

Those who do not plan to vote said that since they have no interest in politics and no knowledge of what is going on, it would be most irresponsible of them to vote. Note that in general less than half of Japanese in their early 20s vote. The second question confirmed the view that few young Japanese care about politics or even read a newspaper. The general sentiment is that they feel that politics is not at all relevant to their lives.

Politicians are perceived by these people as being focused on their own power and enrichment. Politicians may talk about the need for political reform, a better environment, economic reform and more social welfare, but that is nothing but rhetoric. Instead, nothing gets done. The political parties were likened to small groups of old men who kept shifting their affiliations by continually joining and leaving coalitions. "We never know who is in and out of power." Parties change their stances at will. There were complaints that many Soka Gakkai people had supported its own party, the Komeito, which promised to challenge the ideology of the ruling conservatives and that now the Komeito had abandoned its supporters by joining the conservative ruling coalition. One student said it best: "I don't like politicians because they tell lies all the time. I wouldn't vote for any of them. And none of the parties has a sense of mission or any sense of where they want to take Japan."

The less apathetic students said that the future of Japan rests with the quality of its leaders and that they would vote and work for leaders who had a clear purpose to "save the nation" from its current downward economic spiral. Beyond the current economic crisis, there was little consensus on the major issues. Many students said that the quality of the environment and global warming concerned them the most. There is concern that Japan is contributing too much pollution and creating too much unrecycled garbage. Others said that the government must work hard to create more jobs for young people, and two noted that more needed to be done to stop the decline in births in Japan (which after 2007 will lead to an overall population decline)—but nobody suggested support for more immigration. A couple mentioned the question of Japan's flag and national song. A number of students remarked on the recent resignation and indictment of Osaka's disgraced former governor, Knock Yokoyama. One said how incredible it was that the words of a 21-year-old college student were enough to bring down this once hugely popular governor.

This survey did not sample any of the many young Japanese who do not attend college. If anything, these less-educated young Japanese vote less and are even more ignorant of public affairs than their better-educated peers. The Japanese are also very negative in their views on politics. For example. 78.9% feel that politics does not reflect the people's will.

American students are in many respects just as in- different as their Japanese counterparts, but there are always a few students at Mary Baldwin who work actively in campaigns, get involved in causes, or at least join the Young Republicans or Young Democrats on campus. But Japanese students find little if anything appealing about their own parties, which are in fact little more than loose groups of politicians. But my Japanese students were also totally involved in any causes such as the environment.

A group of my American students and I did make a presentation on the forthcoming year 2000 Presidential election in the United States, where we invited Japanese students to express their views on pressing issues in US politics. They did get excited and eagerly expressed their views on such issues as gun control and abortion. At the end of class they overwhelmingly voted for Gore over Bush, even though my American students who participated in the discussion were strong Republicans.

VI. A CASE OF SEXUAL HARASSMENT

We have heard of many cases of sexual harassment in the United States and we all lived through the horrors of the Clinton scandals. Sexual harassment has long been a problem in Japan, but until recently women were told to remain quiet or were too shy or scared to make an issue of harassment. But recently female students and workers have not only started bringing charges against men, but have received more support from university and government authorities.

A famous case of harassment involved former TV comedian turned politician, Knock Yokoyama. Yokoyama was the governor of Osaka Prefecture. He won a landslide victory in 1995 and was re-elected by an impressive margin in April of 1999. A few days before his 1999 election victory, he rode in a campaign car with a twenty-one year-old female campaign volunteer. She alleges that he took certain liberties with her including an attempt to force her legs apart and that he groped her breasts. He denied the charges, declaring that the charges were trumped up with the intention of damaging him politically.

The young woman responded to his charges by filing a damage claim for a considerable sum of money—the modern equivalent of $120,000. He responded with a counter-suit claiming fraud. But when the court began hearing the woman's case, Yokoyama held a news conference where he said that he would not contest the case in court, and while he would pay compensation, he would not admit wrongdoing. He explained that he was far too busy with his job to waste tax payer time fighting this matter in court—that he wanted to settle it and move on.

Yokoyama's response has raised a storm of criticism. Leading newspapers say that if Yokoyama was willing to accept technical guilt against what is really a fairly serious charge, he should resign. The criticism is against his unwillingness to fight the charges as well as his alleged lewd acts.

I asked my advanced writing class of juniors to express their opinions on the matter. Although most of them agreed that Yokoyama had done a good job as governor, if he is not willing to fight the charges and thus admits tacit guilt, he should resign. They expressed anger that a man who represents the public good should try to take advantage of an innocent young woman. A small minority of the students said that one must separate one's public and private lives and that he should continue working on the job that he was elected to. A couple of students wrote how upset they would be if any authority figure including a teacher made advances and one wrote how a high school teacher had once touched her in a sensitive place. Her feelings about Yokoyama were most bitter.

Another class of forty students was evenly divided on the issue. A slight majority of the students, while expressing dismay that Yokoyama was not fighting these charges, said that a charge of sexual harassment, while serious, is a private matter that has little to do with the gentleman's ability to govern. A few students noted the similarities here with the Clinton crisis a year earlier and felt that many Americans had made a similar choice.

In another case involving the alleged rape of a young woman at a Tokyo medical school, while the woman has had difficulty actually proving her charges, the four young male medical students were summarily expelled from the school.

Yokoyama's political career was ruined and he was forced to resign less than a year into his second term. Based on what occurred here, it is clear that women in Japan are beginning to assert their rights and that politicians and other powerful men who used to exploit women shamelessly can no longer get away with such behavior. It is a major advance for women in Japan.

VIII. A GROWING INDIFFERENCE TO AIDS

AIDS is rarely addressed in the Japanese press and many young Japanese interviewed by this writer show little knowledge and outward concern about this killer disease. A 1999 article in the Japanese magazine *SPA!!* presents evidence to support this view:

Frost-haired and pink-cheeked, they tower over us, goddesses on platform shoes. Have cell phones, will travel. What them worry? 'I only do it with Japanese, so its no problem,' says Asuka,18. "I have confidence in my luck" chimes in Mihoko, 21. 'If I get AIDS,' smiles Kimiko, also 21, 'I won't say anything to anybody; I will slip off somewhere by myself, take lots of medicine, and get well.

These amazing statements are not about the common cold, but, rather, a deadly killer disease that afflicts some 25 million people worldwide. The incidence of AIDS is quite small so far in Japan—the Ministry of Health and Welfare reported last in December 1998 that there were 5,633 *reported* cases of AIDS in Japan and that more than 1,000 Japanese had died from complications of AIDS, including some 400 hemophiliacs who died from transfusions of government-approved, AIDS contaminated blood before 1996. Though small, the incidence of AIDS is rising rapidly in Japan and may hit 16,000 by 2003.

Much of this increase is due to the ignorance and naiveté of young Japanese. Not long ago only a small number of high school age Japanese engaged in premarital sex, but today sex has become as common as in the West. A multiple-choice questionnaire done by 100 16-23-year-old women for *SPA!!* showed shocking ignorance of the basic facts of life. Many respondents said that they were safe from AIDS if the boy withdrew just prior to ejaculation. Many respondents say that they know and trust their various partners to be safe—so why use a condom when it feels so good the natural way! Imagine youth so young that even fear of the dread disease is swept aside by the anticipation of a pleasure lasting no more than a heartbeat or two!! There are only two words to describe this:

Innocence and Ignorance. It is clear that sex education is very badly done in Japan and that the result might be catastrophic since premarital sex is rising so rapidly. My own students tell me that what little they know about sex comes from friends or articles in the media. While I never ask anybody about their own private sex lives, one hears through the grape-vine that Japanese men don't like using condoms and that Japanese condoms are in any case very poorly made and breakable.

Another related problem is the almost total lack of testing facilities for AIDS. Most AIDS tests are administered at local health centers where operating hours are limited and privacy is given scant regard. The only solely AIDS testing center is located in a hard-to-reach part of Tokyo and is open for only a few hours a week.

Although AIDS is a minor problem in Japan compared the U.S. and other nations in the West or Africa, it could well become a major problem if young Japanese do not take the threat seriously.

IX. THE FLAG AND DEMOCRACY IN JAPAN

The question of the roles of the Emperor and the people in government became a matter of intense debate during the summer of 1999 when the government introduced a bill that would legislate the Hinomaru ("Rising Sun") as the national flag and Kimigayo as the official national anthem. Both the flag and anthem had been used officially before and during World War II, but had lost official recognition since defeat in 1945. The focus of the debate centered on the modern interpretation of certain words in the national anthem, especially the word *kimi*.

Kimi in traditional Japanese ordinarily means "you," but in some contexts it implies "monarch" or "emperor." Opposition progressive legislators insist that the song and flag are associated with Japan's wartime military campaigns. They point out that Kimigayo was sung

Regularly, until Japan's defeat in the war, for the sake of the Emperor and in hopes that the realm he rules would prosper eternally. The focus, they note, is on the role of the Emperor as ruler of the nation, his official status before 1945, rather than as symbol of the nation, which is how his role is defined in the current American-written constitution, which places sovereignty in the hands of the people.

A broader question is whether the conservative-led government seeks to legally redefine the role of the Emperor and the people—and whether it regards Japan as a democracy whose power resides with the people rather than with the Emperor. Indeed, some opponents of the legislation ask whether this bill, which looks perfectly harmless on paper, is just one more step to undermine the American-sponsored constitution as part of a more general move to return to more statist or authoritarian forms of government and society in Japan.

Recently the government issued a statement saying: "The word kimi in Kimigayo should be interpreted as the Emperor as the symbol of the people." Concerning the entire content of the lyrics, it noted that the song "is a prayer for prosperity and peace in a Japan that holds the Emperor as the symbol of Japan and of the unity of its people."

The newspaper Asahi Shimbun, speaking in opposition to the proposed legislation, countered that the government's explanation of kimi is too strained. "If kimi means the Emperor, then the only possible interpretation of kimigayo is the Emperor's reign. [The phrase] *Chiyo-ni-yachiyo-ni* can only be a prayer for the eternal continuation of his reign....[Indeed,] If kimi means Emperor, it is incompatible with the principle of the sovereignty of the people, the defining principle of the Constitution. It is not surprising that even those who have accepted Kimigayo were skeptical of the government's interpretation....Because the government has tried too hard to find consistency between *Kimigayo*'s eulogy of the Emperor and the principle of the sovereignty of the people, its interpretation of Kimigayo has become even more farfetched."

Today both the Hinomaru and Kimigayo are used in an informal and informal manner, but the government bill would give them legal recognition. A recent poll sponsored by the Japan Broadcasting Corporation (NHK) suggests that there is still considerable public resistance to official legislation of the national flag and national anthem. Most of the respondents said that they were happy with the current unofficial status of both the flag and the anthem; only forty-seven percent supported legislation while thirty-three percent were opposed. The rest (20%) were noncommittal. An Asahi Shimbun poll indicated that two-thirds of the Japanese public opposes hasty passage of the bill so that there could be more discussion of its far-reaching ramifications.

X. AUM AGAIN

[Journal Entry: November 15, 1999]

Aum Shinrikyo has struck again. Headlines in today's *Yomiuri Shimbun* screamed: 2 Aum Members held over Confining Woman. " Aum had proclaimed that it had abandoned its violent practices of the past, but today's news stories describe cells where members who disobey Aum regulations and practices are held in isolation for many days.

Four years ago in March 1995, Aum struck at the Tokyo Subway system at rush hour with poison gas, killing 12, seriously injuring several hundred, and causing harm to another six thousand. Aum's leaders were jailed and several have been sentenced including one sentenced to death. However, many members remained in Aum after the 1995 subway incident, and a number of other younger members have joined since.

Most Japanese show deep hatred for and fear of Aum. Its communes, most of which are located in small cities or semi-rural towns, receive very harsh treatment from local residents who fear that Aum will harm or kill local residents. The Japanese government is under intense pressure to formally ban or dissolve Aum as a distinct threat to public safety, but civil libertarians fear that if Aum is banned, the constitutional provision guaranteeing religious freedom will be meaningless.

Last semester I asked forty of my students to debate the question whether Aum should be banned. One student opposed the proposition, noting that one must protect the civil liberties of people even if we don't like them, but everybody else vehemently supported government action against Aum. They argued that Aum is a terrorist group and not a religious organization and that it therefore is exempt from constitutional provisions protecting genuine religious life. When I commented that religious groups are protected in the US, the students reminded me of the WACO incident in 1993. "At least here in Japan our government does not shoot members of despised sects!"

XI. DEATH PENALTY IN JAPAN

One snowy morning in early 1969 while a student at Waseda University in Tokyo, I was awakened by my Japanese house-mother, who was urgently telling me that there was a police detective wishing to interview me. The officer flashed his wooden badge and informed me that I was a suspect in a string of murders that had occurred in Japan in the previous months. Some person had killed 4 taxi drivers in places ranging from Hokkaido to Tokyo, Nagoya and Kyoto. His American-made gun had been stolen from the US air force base at Tachikawa, near Tokyo, thus leading to the possibility that the killer was an American. Working on that premise, the police looked for foreigners staying in hotels near the crime scenes. My name immediately popped up in Hakadote (Hokkaido). They traced me to Tokyo where I lived near the second scene and noted that I had also gone to Nagoya and Kyoto.

I was told not to leave Tokyo, but was relieved to learn a week later that the *ryokan* owner remembered that my wife and I had definitely been in the *ryokan* at the time of the Hakodate murder. Later a young Japanese man, recently fired as a Tachikawa base worker, was caught in Shibuya (Tokyo) trying to kill driver #5. He was tried at age 19, convicted and sentenced to death by hanging (the method of execution in Japan). He languished on death row until 1996 when he was executed at age 47. By that time he had put himself through college (correspondence courses) and had become a best-selling novelist. His death greatly saddened me.

When I was a suspect in 1969, murders were quite rare in Japan, but crime in general and murder in particular is on the rise now —although it is quite minor by American standards. The recent surge in murders –including 24 or more committed by Aum Shinrikyo—has led to a recent rise in public support for the death penalty.

A poll conducted by the Japanese Prime Minister's office in late 1999 indicates full support for the penalty at 79.3% and strong opposition at 8.8%—the rest were undecided. The previous poll (1994) indicated only about 74% in favor of the death penalty. About 49 percent of those supporting the penalty said it should be maintained because those who commit felonies should pay with their own lives. 48.6% said that families of victims would not feel satisfied until the penalty was carried out. Many also said that keeping murderers alive poses the danger of them murdering again. 54.4% agreed that the penalty is an effective deterrent to crime. Over 30 criminals were executed between 1993 and 2000.

My female students were much more divided on this issue. One student wrote the following essay in opposition:

No, I don't agree with the death penalty because everyone has a right to live. Of course, criminals must atone for their wrong they did. They are penitent and have to become men who are able to contribute to society. By this they pay compensation. The death penalty is immoral. As it is no surprise that victims and their family want to kill criminals, they don't understand when they knew that the criminals were not put to death. However, they can't kill murderers. Murderers consider the way of execution in prison by themselves.…I don't know the difference between the death penalty and life imprisonment.….I don't think that the death penalty decreases more killing (we have the death penalty and yet the rate rises) and crimes, and I think that there are other ways, which is criminals change their mind and regret committing their crimes admitting how wrong their crimes were. I think everybody can change their minds, victims and murderers alike."

Another student, writing in support of the penalty, noted:

First of all, by committing crimes, criminals give a great damage to a victim, a victim's family and society. Criminals who commit felonies (murder) should compensate with their own lives. Otherwise, victims or victim's families' rights wouldn't be respected. Secondly, the death penalty can prevent more possible felonies....

The death penalty debate in Japan strongly resembles its American counterpart.

XII. CIVIL RIGHTS FOR GAYS IN JAPAN

There was an article on the editorial page of my hometown newspaper, The [Staunton, Virginia] *Daily News Leader*, in early January 2000 which lauded the recent Vermont State Supreme Court decision granting legal rights to gay couples. The court based its decision on the premise that since the Constitution grants full rights to all people, to grant certain privileges to heterosexual couples and to deny these same rights to gay couples is both unconstitutional and inhuman. The Court mandated the Vermont Legislature to pass laws granting the same rights to gay couples as heterosexuals. This matter is of acute personal interest to me. I made civil rights for gays the centerpiece in my election campaign in 1997 for the Virginia State Legislature[26] and must salute the Vermont court for its wisdom. I

---

[26] I ran as a Green Party candidate against the Speaker of the Virginia House, Vance Wilkins, a Republican, receiving 17% of the vote.

also xeroxed the article and handed it to my Japanese students in several classes in Kyoto.

My students, a motley crew of female freshmen, sophomores and juniors, were fascinated with the issue and several lively debates ensued. The students informed me that issues pertaining to homosexuality are rarely if ever discussed in Japan, even in private. Unlike the US, Japanese gays stay strictly in the closet because to come out might lead to embarrassment and ridicule. They noted that there is no acceptable place for gays in Japanese society and that openly gay people might have difficulty in finding work and housing. This article was the first time many of the students had even heard of the concept of gay marriage and they seemed interested, but puzzled. They all stated that they had never discussed the gay issue in class and that discussing homosexuality was almost taboo in Japanese culture.

The general response to the question whether gay relationships in Japan should receive the same legal rights accorded to heterosexual couples was very mixed. Virtually all of the students with boy friends said that the boy friends would find a gay relationship to be "gross," "disgusting," or "unnatural." The females, however, were in general a bit more sympathetic. They all agreed that what people do in private is their own personal business and most said they had never met anyone who is gay ("We in Japan have far fewer gay people than in America."). Most, but by no means all, felt that it is only fair for gay couples to have equal legal rights, but the idea of gay marriage made many of them feel quite uncomfortable. They agreed that gays are human and that their rights and lives should be protected. But, above all, most were surprised to learn that in America gays were "coming out" and seeking rights. That, they all noted, would be impossible in Japan because most people are "not enlightened."

XIII. A QUESTION OF DEBT

The high cost of education combined with the poor economy has resulted in many Japanese students being burdened by debt by the time they graduate from university. After graduation some will spend up to 20 years paying back student loans. Take the case of Taro (pseudonym), a freshman at a private university in Tokyo. Despite the fact that he cuts school expenses by living at home with his parents, he has been forced to take out nearly 5 million yen ($US48 thousand in 1999) in student loans which he will begin paying back immediately upon graduation. He receives about 80,000 yen a month in loans ($780) from the Japan scholarship foundation, which carry interest. In addition, his parents paid about Yen 1 million ($9800) to pay for his university admission fees. They are also making interest payments on some of his loans while he is in school. After graduation, Taro will make payments of Yen 50,000 ($480) a month for 20 years—totaling 6.3 million yen (($62,000).

Taro's father is an office worker who earns a decent salary, but he has an ailing mother to take care of and his financial situation is tight. While Japanese parents have traditionally paid for their children's education, because of the recession, an increasing number of parents can no longer do so. Today 25% of the families who have children living at home and attending university are forced to borrow money from banks. In cases where children live away from home while in college, the figure rises to 28%.

The fact that many students choose to work 5-6 hours a day to avoid taking out loans means that they have much less time to study. Some students find the burden of debt to be much too hard to shoulder and declare bankruptcy, especially those who have trouble finding work in a tight economy. The burden imposed by the school loans is changing the relationship between parents and children.... According to one official, "There are many parents who are chagrined because they cannot do anything for their children."

According to another article, young women college graduates lucky enough to get office jobs in big cities have a hard time. The average 23-year-old secretary working in a medium-sized firm earns slightly less than $2,000 a month. She pays $600-800 in rent for a minute apartment, $300-400 in various taxes, $100 for utilities, $200plus for transportation, leaving only about $500 for very expensive food and other daily expenses. If she has a college loan of $400, she must skip meals and all forms of pleasure—and keep her heat to a minimum. Saving money is impossible. She may seek a boy friend who can take her out for a good meal or a rare movie.

The vast majority of my students at my Kyoto college come from hard hit middle-class families. Most of the students work one or two part-time jobs at 7-11, Pizza

Hut or elsewhere at $7.80 an hour just to get by. In better times many of our students apply to study abroad for a year or to go on a summer trip. In 1998, 26 students applied for foreign study at various sister-schools abroad——this year the figure was 12.

Tough economic times may not have curbed the appetite of Japanese for short trips abroad, but the higher costs of long-term foreign travel and study have made it increase-ingly difficult for young Japanese to experience a non-tourist's view of life abroad. Study abroad was one way that younger Japanese since the 1960s had permeated their nation's true isolation from the outside world.

Section III

Life Off Campus

While Section II dealt with students' views on a variety of issues affecting Japanese and foreign cultures, Section III examines various aspects of the lives of young Japanese women away from school and the major political issues of the day.

I. HANDY-PHONE CULTURE IN JAPAN

Japan seems to have little use for some aspects of the new information age. Standing on the threshold of the information era, Japan seems frozen. Although the number of Japanese on-line is growing (those saying they had no access dropped from 69.2% in 1997 to 61.9% in 1998), it is still the worst among the developed nations....The wireless boom is changing Japan's online population, but a 1999 Dentsu survey shows that access alone is not the answer. Across the board Japanese have low expectations of the benefits to be reaped from new technology. In every nation more than 50% of all respondents said that they saw access to information from around the world as a benefit of information technology. But only in Japan was that the only benefit. Less than half (46.3%) thought it would make work more efficient. Slightly less (45%) thought it would stimulate

75

the than a quarter (22%) said it would make life more convenient through on-line shopping; one-fifth (20.3%) felt it would create more business opportunities. Dentsu analysts argue that Japanese seem to be uncertain as to how and for what ends they should utilize the fruits of information technology to renovate and organize the social system.[27]

When I asked my many students in Kyoto to write an essay on what they would place in a time capsule that would best describe Japan in 2000 to future generations of

Japanese centuries in the future, roughly half the students responded that they would include their "handy-phones." This was hardly surprising since it would be very hard to find a student without one of these tiny gadgets in their possession at all times.

A survey published in the *Japan Times* indicates that roughly 50% of all Japanese (any age) owns one of these personal telephones. Indeed, a few people have gone so far as to criticize me for not having one of these new-fangled inventions. These phones make it possible for people anywhere in Japan to reach you at any time. I must admit that they are handy when I am meeting a person and have lost my way or am running late, but they are a nuisance when you simply want to be left alone. More Japanese have a handy-phone number than for Americans to have any kind of E-mail address.

Japan has become very much of a handyphone culture. When I arrived in Japan in March, 1999, I was amazed to see people walking down the streets seemingly conversing to no one—only to realize that they had these tiny phones clutched to their ears. Now when you crowd on trains or push through school corridors, you see myriads of people bellowing into these

---

[27] *Japan Times,* December 4, 1999, p. 6.

tiny machines. When you ride the Shinkansen bullet trains, the conductors politely request that any person making or receiving calls please do so in standing areas between cars. This is a necessary request because you are privy to other people's calls even when you are taking a quiet stroll in the park.

Right now, Japan is in the grips of a digital revolution unlike anything the world has ever seen or experienced. While the United States forged the first path through the hi-tech jungle, it is now still struggling to free itself from a hard-wired, network-based computer-centered environment that still depends on antiquated machines and software.

Japan, as it has done so often in the past, has surged ahead. It has largely by-passed the first (mainframe) and second (desktop) generations of the digital

Revolution and is implementing a third (wireless) phase of the revolution. It was common to see my students not only calling each other frequently, but also sending and receiving e-mails as well by phone.

A Tokyo-based writer noted recently:

The extraordinarily rapid spread of handy-phones affords a clear opportunity to see how and why the Japanese are winning the global battle for digital supremacy. Elsewhere in the world, including the United States and northern Europe, clever engineers started with the idea of miniaturizing the cumbersome telephone, which they did with commendable success. But Japanese designers began with a different idea—they started with the all-purpose notion of a handheld device and then asked, "What can we make it do?" The phone part was the obvious starting point, but now other functions have begun to appear: personal information management, online games, graphics displays of mini-photo albums, global positioning readouts, financial services. Scarcely a week goes by without another innovation. Two-way video-phones are currently advertised on all the subways. And there's one phone that even can transmit your temperature, heart-rate and blood pressure to a central medical databank while you use it. The overwhelming success story has been the Internet phone-Web-based computer telephones that by-pass traditional long-distance telephone charges–which has spread faster than the industry's own optimistic projections.[28]

When I asked my largest class of 39 students how many of them owned and carried around handyphones, everybody's hand went up. It seems that there are few if any teenagers in Japan without these items. It is indeed possible to turn them off, but quite often students forget and they ring in class—my policy was that students must answer and carry on a conversation in English. (In fact, these little monsters never ring—they buzz, play musical tunes like Yankee-Doodle Dandy, or vibrate. Train conductors request that passengers put the phones in vibration mode.)

The handyphone business is very intense in Japan, so much so that various phone companies are literally giving away phones to potential subscribers. The basic costs are also quite modest, but if you talk as much as some of my own students do, you have to get a part-time job (or second-part-time job) to pay the monthly fee.

The contrast between American and Japanese students at KWC was notable. The Americans were very much into E-Mail culture, but felt isolated from the handy-phone world. Very few Japanese use E-mail since only about 10% of Japanese homes (as opposed to 35% in the US) have personal computers.

Japanese simply have not fully joined the world of pcs and the internet and thus seem to be very far behind the US in this area. It is said, however, that Japanese are perfecting the use of handyphones in doing e-mail and other computer functions which will jump-start them back into the technology race.

---

[28] David Wade, "Tokyo Technoculture" in *Hemisphere* (December 2000), p. 118.

We live in a very interesting world.

II. NON-CONFORMIST YOUTH STREET MUSICIANS ARE A RAY OF SUNSHINE

Most Japanese young people are conformist and follow the mainstream dream of school, career and marriage, but as in any culture there is a strong minority that is quite unwilling to conform to the norm. The tragedy is that Japan has no really open avenue for non-conformists, so they seek an escape valve such as the Street Beat or by joining cults like Aum Shinrikyo....The people I inter-viewed during my Aum research do not sound all that different from the street musicians. The Aum faithful joined a cult to escape the rigors and pressurized misery of Japanese life while street musicians seek personal freedom.

It was fun to observe and talk to many young street musicians, often boys and girls in their late teens. Even a few of my students said that they played music on the street on occasion. The following piece is based on an article published in the *Mainichi Dail News* in November, 1999.

An old man, slightly drunk, approaches unsteadily. "Give us a song," he says. He tosses a thousand yen bill ($10 US) into the box. Ken Nakazawa, his guitar case cushioning him from the concrete floor, nods his thanks and obliges. The song is his own composition. It proceeds to the accompaniment of trains and footsteps.

Shinjuku Station is not Suntory Hall. Nakazawa does not expect it to be. He's 23, and has been playing venues like this for 3 years. The song ends...The old man's face is wreathed in a smile. "Very nice! I like a young man like you. A young man with pluck. Yes, but...." His face turns sad.

"But What?" asks Nakazawa. The man emerges from his reverie. His smile returns. He shakes his head. "No," he says, "my son...I would not want my son doing this."

Would he want his daughter doing it? Hiroko Sato is 17 and you will find her Monday nights under Ikebukuro Station. She starts at 10pm and sometimes, when the feeling is right and the force with her, she plays all night, going straight to school the next morning. A year ago she came to Tokyo from rural Tochigi Prefecture to attend high school. She had never seen a street musician before…The first one she encountered impressed her. There's something about a young person with a guitar that strikes you even before you have passed judgment on the music. Hiroko's first thought sums it up to perfection: "I wonder if I could do that!"

Slowly, she decided that she could, though she had never been musical. Never mind, she would learn. Three months later she was at We Road with a guitar and two songs she had written. A passing business man stopped to listen. His verdict was blunt—"You can't sing and you can't play—but keep trying." And he fumbled in his pocket for some change. Hiroko checked him. "I am not doing this for money." "I know" said the businessman, pressing the coins on her anyway. "Think of it this way; I'm betting on you. More than that, I am entrusting my dream to you."

Cryptic words. Maybe something of what they mean is embodied in another musician, Yuji Otake, whose age, 33, sets him somewhat apart from younger members of the street singer tribe. Otake grew up wanting to be a musician. He played guitar young, but his bandmates all got jobs and his parents had certain expectations. He went to college, majored in political science and became a successful accountant, but the yearning for music would never leave. Finally he quit his job and took to the streets where he remains 3 yrs later.

What is beguiling about these musicians is that even among the more serious and talented ones, few are really interested in successful recording careers. They live for now and disregard agents who pass out business cards. They live for one song at a time. And money? Many street musicians have part-time jobs, but Otake doesn't and is happy about that. He wants music to be his livelihood as well as his life. He hopes to attract a music group for an outside concert with many in the crowd paying them something. The emphasis seems to be on self-expression, which means doing their own songs and living life as they want it.

A last stop on our musical tour is Kichioji in the far western suburbs of Tokyo. The players are Shogo Isobe and Motonari Takami, both 27. They grew up together in Hamamatsu in Shizuoka Prefecture and learned guitar as kids. Later they moved together to Tokyo, rooming together in a one-room flat that afforded them 3-mats each!! They played on the streets at trendy Harajuku and they have become so good over 8 years that a CD debut is pending. Another aspect of the situation is summed up by a young man from Fukuoka. New to Tokyo, he was wandering alone one day last spring when he happened upon the pair performing at their latest venue in front of Kichioji station. Here was music to warm a lost soul. At intermission, he struck up a conversation with the musicians. "They were my first Tokyo friends," he smiles.

III. VALENTINES IN JAPAN

It was the week before Valentine's Day in Kyoto and a large department store, Takashimaya, was having a special on chocolate for Valentine's Day. Even though it was a normal work day, at lunch time the special Valentine's sales area was filled with young and middle-aged women buying up expensive boxes of chocolate for the men in their lives. There were a few Valentine's cards on the racks, but nobody was paying them any heed.

Japanese associate Valentine's with chocolate and more chocolate. The average Japanese consumes about 1.1 kg. of chocolate per year (the average America downs five times that much and the average Swiss/German gobbles 10 kg—I am Swiss/German by heritage and follow their chocolate traits), but sixty percent of that modest total is consumed around Valentine's Day.

Japan is the world's ultimate materialist consumer society, so it is hardly surprising that corporate Japan invented a way to get TWO Valentine's days. The traditional February date is the time when women *give* and men *receive*. In addition, there is a "White" Valentine's Day in mid-March when men are supposed to reciprocate. One of my former Japanese students told me recently that she spends a small fortune buying her boyfriend chocolate and a tie for Valentine's each year only to be is told in March that he has "forgotten." She says that there are times when he is very self-centered. That makes her very angry.

The price for flowers in the US is considerably higher than in Japan, especially on Valentine's Day, but Japanese lovers rarely give each other flowers, even on February 14th. Nor do many Japanese send each other Valentine's cards.

The ultimate gift is a box of Godaiva chocolates—a big box of which sells for $35 in the US, but $90-100 in Japan. It is said that if a woman gives you even a small batch of Godaiva chocolate, she is really in love with you.

Valentine's (or the closest week-end) is also a time when sweethearts go out for a full-scale meal. The biggest romantic night at a restaurant is Christmas Eve (the boy friend of my former student mentioned above paid $290 for a blast at their favorite fancy Italian eatery), but Valentine's is a close second.

IV. A GEISHA ENCOUNTER

One night my departmental chair kindly invited me to join him on a foray into Kyoto's Gion district to eat some good food and visit his favorite bar. It's located in the very old part of the Gion, next to a bridge and a pure stream where I take all first-time visitors to Kyoto as the start of our tour. The buildings in the Gion district date back to the late Edo period (early 19th century).

The evening was continuing in a very pleasant but quiet manner when around 10:00 a fully-dressed *maiko* (young woman apprentice-geisha) came in and chatted playfully with all the guests. She was dressed in a full white and gold

Kimono, white face make-up, and a very fancy hair-do that one sees in ancient prints of Japanese women.

Japan honors its past traditions. Old temples are beautifully cared for and ancient sports such as sumo are still popular. The geisha represent an old art form which recognizes the subservient yet almost beguiling nature of women who entertain men.

This young woman strolled confidently into the bar, posed for pictures with male patrons at each table, and engaged in small-talk with each group. Then the attractive young woman of 19 or so finally came to our table and posed for her umpteenth picture of the evening. But being a good Japanologist, I seized the moment to ask her about being a geisha in Kyoto.

The *maiko* said that the Geisha profession is in slow decline. There are only about 300 active geisha in Kyoto now and perhaps 50 maiko in training. She, like all other *maiko*, began her training right after graduating from middle school, when she moved into a special house whose owner and staff train the *maiko* for the life of a geisha. The house pays for all the training and living expenses of the *maiko*, but the future geisha must repay these costs later through her own earnings.

There are two kinds of geisha—those who sing and play instruments such as the samisen—and those who specialize in dance. My temporary companion was training to be a dancer.

A geisha is a highly trained artist who performs at a variety of events including private or corporate parties for businessmen. But the training of a geisha involves a lot more than mere art. A maiko learns all about good manners, and polite conversation and how to flatter male company. A geisha who joins a group of businessmen at their table in a restaurant or bar is like a human taxi with her meter running—except that she is far more expensive (about $100 an hour).

A geisha is also a businesswoman who can earn big money and who must do so to pay back all of her maiko training expenses. A successful geisha also often needs a male sponsor who will invest money and time in her—but I am not sure what if any return he gets. Our *maiko* said that it's very hard to find sponsors today—mainly because of the recession—which means that increasing numbers of *maiko* are not becoming geisha. She noted, however, that like any other traditional art form in Japan, the geisha tradition will continue.

What do geisha do when they get older? When we left around 11 p.m., I was quickly introduced to the "mamasan" in her fifties who owns the bar. She told me that she too had once been a Geisha, but she wondered if there was a future for today's *maiko* in a Japan where today's youth is moving away from traditional values.

V. LOVE AND MARRIAGE MEET THE BOY FRIENDS

There is plenty of evidence of the increasing liberation of Japanese women. One area where they seem to derive their own pleasures is in having a multiplicity of boy friends.

Nuclear plants leak, Shinkansen train tunnels crumble, and 30,000 Japanese committed suicide in 1998. That's the bad news. The good news is that there are other things to talk about. Would you believe it? One young woman in three is having an affair behind her boyfriend's or husband's back. Yes, says SPA, women in their teens and 20s are super light when it comes to what used to be known by the grimly disapproving and darkly horrified word "fornication." Not all women, of course. Statistics bend according to the weight you give them. *SPA!'s* survey of 160 women yields 35% who habitually sleep with men other than their regular partners (which means that 65% don't!!).

Moreover, among those who do, 57% claim to be haunted by constant guilt.[29] *SPA!* reported the following:

Whether guilt disqualifies the young libertarians from super lightness, or whether their failures to modify their behavior lends the word added pertinence, is an open question which given the super lightness of the occasion, we will decline to get bogged down in. Let us instead turn to five women SPA profiles as representatives of the flighty generation. Their names have been changed to protect their innocence.

I want my boyfriend thinking about me all the time," says Kaori who at 24 claims to have shared beds with 15 men. "But he's so busy at work, and I hate to be a burden on him." Interesting: She makes the dark side of her double life seems like a sacrifice to her boyfriend's peace of mind. If you're lonely in your boyfriend's absence, SPA suggests, can't you get together with a girlfriend? Kaori sighs, "Hanging around with women tires me. Only a man can dispel the loneliness I feel when I can't be with my boyfriend. And it's nice—I get a free meal, he picks me up in his car." Under persistent questioning, she grows petulant. "But men sleep around, don't they?" SPA cannot deny that they do. "Besides," she continues, "its not just sex. I like to be pampered by men. And it doesn't hurt my boyfriend. He doesn't suspect a thing. I'm real good at alibis. If he doesn't know, it's as if it's not happening."

Amen, says Eri. Eri's 28, a stewardess. Romantic? It's supposed to be, but her dream is to say good-bye to all that and become a housewife. And she has a boyfriend whose housewife she wants to be. Trouble is that she is making more money than he is. They can't possibly set up housekeeping on his salary. That's what keeps her in the air and she's not happy about it. Does she feel guilty, *SPA!* asks, about her one night stands in Los Angeles, New York and Rome? "Absolutely not," she replies. "Is it my fault his wages are so low?" Besides, having men at your feet who dress you up and take you to first-class restaurants is not a pleasure to be thrown over lightly.

Not to mention sex, which is important if you are a stewardess. "It relieves flight stress," she says. "I've tried everything—aromatherapy, healing music,. Nothing works like sex. You should try it!!"

Yuriko, an office worker, knows somebody else who should try it. At 25, she's been going out with the same guy for 5 years and so far as she knows, he's still a virgin. Not her, mind you!! She took measure of their sexless "spiritual relationship" three years ago, and

has had five lovers since. What's her man's problem? Not knowing he has one, apparently. But "I'm an ordinary woman!" she laments to *SPA!*. "I have sexual feelings!" Why not leave him then? "Because he's so nice to talk to. Sex isn't everything."

No sex isn't everything, agrees Aiko, 19. Revenge counts for a great deal. When she was 17, she learned that her boyfriend was playing the field. She decided to get back on her own and has been doing it with gusto ever since. Her rage calmed, she sails serenely out in search of alternate pleasures like soft S&M, which is nice, but a little too kinky for a serious relationship.

Only one of *SPA!*'s quintet of liberated women is married. Yuki, 27, has had quite a career. She figures she had 30 men before her marriage at 24, and 20 after, and she's still young. She hopes her cunning will flower with age. It had better. Her husband has already caught her three times. By turns tearful and violent, he has always forgiven so far, but his temperament seems unpredictable, and right now Yuki is being very careful with her three beaux, not least because they too are married!! Of course its hard on a husband, she says, but what can a girl do? Her husband is kind and attentive, and a good lover besides

her favorite, but "a woman likes to be told she's beautiful," and husbands grow notoriously weary of paying compliments. She has a child too, and "I don't particularly dislike motherhood" any more than she dislikes wifehood," but "I want to be seen as a woman!"

Kaori, whom we met earlier, is taking time off from her erotic roving. She's gotten fat, she says. It's made her shy. No, she'll stay at home for a while and think about life, toting up its pluses and minuses. She already has an idea. "Japan," she says, "should allow bigamy." Then she laughs and winks at SPA's reporter. "You know," she says, "if you weren't on assignment, I could go for you."

LOVE, MARRIAGE, CAREERS AND FAMILY

Japan used to be very much a marrying society. Virtually everybody got married in prewar Japan, and it was extremely rare to meet somebody who was not married. Of course, within certain professions, marriage was rare; priests in some Buddhist sects and women who worked as *geisha*. It was also uncommon for a woman to have both a professional career and a family. There were a few career women in the Meiji era (1868-1912), but the idea that a woman could pursue an active career outside the home while raising a family remains controversial even today. Postwar Japanese women through the 1980s could have a career in certain fields if they chose, but these women rarely if ever married while pursuing their careers.

When I questioned many of my Japanese students in 1999-2000 about their futures, virtually everybody said that she hoped to work for a few years, most likely in an office of a larger corporation. Very few expressed any illusions that they might advance in their careers in the office to become administrators or even executives. Rather, they saw themselves as becoming OLs ("Office Ladies" or busy secretaries and office assistants) who would work for a few years before finding the right man, marrying him and raising a family. A few stated that they had loftier goals—some dreamed of becoming airline stewardesses with all the romance of travel and time spent abroad. They were stunned when I told them that very few Americans had much admiration or respect for a job such as a steward or stewardess. A few others admitted dreams of becoming teachers or even artists or musicians, but only one expressed any interest in such traditional professions as law, medicine, college teaching or business management.

Indeed, the idea of a professional career did not even register in the minds of any of my Japanese students. This is in marked contrast to my students at Mary Baldwin college, virtually all of whom state a desire for a career or at least an interesting and profitable job. When I survey my American students every year, it is rare to find even one student who will admit that her single life goal is to become a housewife and to raise children. But an overwhelming majority of my Japanese students stated that their main goal in life was to become a nurturing and loving wife and mother. A freshman in KWC's now defunct junior college said: "You say that every woman should seek a profession and become a professional person, but in reality it is much better if we stay home and take care of our families. In truth, there is no more important job in life than being a mother. A good mother must stay at home to care for her children. In comparison, it is selfish to go out and seek a career when you have children."

I distributed a survey to my 230 students asking them about their marriage and career plans and whether they planned a more traditional "arranged" marriage or a more contemporary "love" marriage where the choices would be made by the partners themselves. The responses indicated that virtually all the young women planned to marry; only five students said that they didn't plan to marry because they wished to have the freedom to live their lives on their terms and did not want to have the restrictions that any marriage partnership would impose on them. One of these respondents said that she wanted to have children outside of wedlock, and all five said that they regarded marriage to be a form of slavery which would deprive them of their personal freedom. Virtually none of the students wanted to get married before the age of 25; most said that the best age would be between 28-30 with many opting for age 30 or later. After marriage they hoped for two children, although a few wanted as many as four.

There were many reasons offered for the desire to delay marriage. The students said that since they would spend the rest of their years rearing children, they first wanted five to ten years to first live on their own. They wanted the opportunity to support themselves, to live alone, and to be truly independent before they had to surrender these privileges.

The greatest quality young women want in their potential boyfriends and husbands is kindness–a cooperative spirit where men are genuinely helpful and care about the welfare of their beloved. I was told constantly by my students that they were looking for male companions who would help in the care of the household and respect them as individuals. A surprisingly large minority, however, said that they wanted their husbands to be rich so that they themselves could enjoy their lives while their mates busied themselves at work.

The freshmen, sophomores and juniors I taught in Kyoto had far less experience with men than most of my students at Mary Baldwin. An anonymous survey indicates that only a quarter of my freshmen and sophomores would admit to any sexual experience[30] and only about thirty percent had steady boy friends. Only about half had dated by age 20 and most admitted that they were inexperienced when it came to relationships with men of any age outside of their families.

All of the respondents understood the cultural tradition of arranged marriages, but none wished for one themselves. They all wanted love marriages, whereby they would find their own mates and experience a courtship that was based on their own terms. They would resort to an arranged marriage only if they failed to find mates when they were young.

When it came to the question of whether they would marry a man who met the opposition of their parents, a small handful noted that they would marry the man of their choice no matter what! "We live in a society where we are guaranteed freedom of choice and I expect my parents to honor my judgment of the man in my life absolutely." But over eighty percent of the respondents said that they could not marry against their parents' wishes. Family is very important to them, and they would not oppose their parents even if it meant not marrying the man of their dreams. Most said that if their parents opposed their choices, they would work hard to convince their parents to know and appreciate their male partner.

One student, speaking for the majority, noted: "My parents brought me into the world and have raised me. Keeping close to the family—maintaining family unity is far more important than any marriage." Another noted that the family was the key to life in Japan, that the family mattered far more than the individual selfish desires of any one member. One reminded me that her family honored its ancestors and if she somehow lost her family, she could no longer be close to the ancestors and family. Several had boyfriends that they knew would be objectionable to their parents and family, so the romances remained very secret. One very objectionable relationship for parents would be having their daughters marry foreigners—one girl with an Italian-American boyfriend ruefully notes that she knows that they can never marry because of how her parents feel—thus, the relationship remains secret. [31]

SURVEY OF 230 FEMALE STUDENTS CONCERNING LOVE AND MARRIAGE

Do you think you will marry some day: Yes 94% No: 6%

Assuming you do marry, what age?:

Before 25:   26%

26-28 :   30%

28-30 :   30%

30+ :   10%

Unsure :   4%

Do you want a love or traditional marriage:

Love :   96%

Traditional: 4%

Would you ever date a foreigner?:

Yes: 50%

No :   50%

---

31 The student wrote me a year later that she had given up her foreign boy friend. "He is a nice man, but I dated him not so much for his attraction as for the chance to see what it is like to be with a foreign man. When the novelty wore off, the attraction was gone."

Marry a foreigner:

Yes :   30%

No :   70%

Would you marry a man your parents disapprove of?

Yes :   40%

No :   60%

Another telling change is the refusal of many younger women to fulfill the traditional role of "*oyome-san*" or daughter-in law. Traditionally, three generations of one family lived together, and the daughter-in-law was responsible for the care of her in-laws as well as the maintenance of the household. However, this system has declined in recent years, especially in urban areas.

As young couples have left home, the number of elderly people living on their own has skyrocketed. Seniors aged 65 and older today account for almost 46 percent of households in Japan, compared with less than 20 percent in 1972. Over the same period, the number of three-generation families living under one roof has declined from 55.8 percent to 29.7 percent. Most of the remaining extended families live in small cities or towns or in farm regions, but even here they are rapidly declining.[32] The reasons for this decline are many–the lure of cities, the desire of more women to work outside the house, and, most importantly, the fact that younger women no longer want to live in such a subservient role.

---

[32] Stephanie Strom, "On the Rise in Japan: Assertive Daughters-in-Law" in *The New York Times,* 22 April, 2001.

A Matter of Divorce

Divorce has become a fairly common phenomenon in Japan. The divorce rate was only one in twenty as recently as the late 1960s, but today as many as a third of all marriages fail, and the number is increasing rapidly. Divorce is especially common among couples in the 45-56 age range. Women in this age group are more commonly working, are capable of supporting themselves, and have an "empty nest" at home. This greater independence makes them less reliant on their husbands, who in turn are increasingly less patient with their "uppity" wives.

A number of students at the college wrote about their divorced parents. The most common complaint of their mothers is that their husbands were rarely home and truly married to their jobs. Their fathers complained that the mothers too often had jobs or careers that removed them from the support roles women had once played at home.

The growing possibility of divorce makes young women all the more apprehensive about marriage. Traditional arranged marriages led to very few divorces, but increased freedom and more love marriages puts the responsibility for the success of the marriages in the hands of the couples themselves. Japanese women are very proud of their newfound freedoms, and there is a growing feeling among some that marriage is a definite threat to this liberty.

CAN IT BE TRUE? JAPANESE PREFER GIRLS?

Demographic experts have expressed deep reservations recently about population trends in such countries as India, China, South Korea and Taiwan. There, abortions of female fetuses, particularly among women who already have one girl, are blamed for creating a large surplus of males, a population imbalance that could prove socially de-stabilizing when the boys grow up and find that there are not enough girls to marry. In China, there are now 118 boys per 100 girls under age 5. In South Korea, despite the introduction of harsh penalties for doctors caught per-forming prenatal gender screenings, by 1999 there were 110 male births per 100 female (down from 117 in 1990), and a recent study estimated that about 30,000 female fetuses were aborted that year. Statistics suggest that half of all female fetuses conceived in families that already had two children were aborted. The ratio of boys to girls in Taiwan in 1990 was 110-100. In Japan, however, 105.4 boys were born last year for every 100 girls, a ratio statistically unchanged since 1899 and matching the global norm.

Why the discrepancy between Japan and its East Asian neighbors? One factor, according to a recent survey in Japan, is that young Japanese couples today, in a stunning repudiation of the traditional Asian values that have placed a premium on producing male heirs, prefer girls by a margin of 3-1. Daughters are seen as cuter, easier to handle, more emotionally accessible, and, even more importantly in this fast-aging society, more likely to look after their elderly parents.

Plenty of Japanese are dubious about whether the current crop of female infants will grow up to fulfill their parents' hopes, but a passion for baby girls has spawned hot-selling books and magazines, pricey new personalized advice services for sex selection, and clinics dispensing suppository jelly—pink to help produce girls or green for boys—for would-be parents trying to conceive the child of their dreams.

One twenty-seven-year-old housewife, Yamaguchi Yumi, notes, "Boys don't listen and are harder to raise." To improve her odds of conceiving a girl, Yamaguchi has scrupulously followed the advice in a popular sex-selection book and took her temperature for an entire year before trying to become pregnant. She sobbed with joy when her daughter Ami was born in 1998. "Boys and their mothers seem to have a weak bond, but mothers and daughters stay close all of their lives." Their joy might have been very different as recently as 1980 when such couples usually hoped for a boy to carry on the family business and name.

The Sex Selection Study Association of Japan, which has 800 obstetricians as members, estimates that only 2% of Japanese women seeking to conceive are taking measures to select the baby's gender—and that so far there has been no appreciable change in the sex ratio of Japanese newborns. That may be because sex-selective abortion is unheard of in Japan. Though abortion is legal through the 22nd week of pregnancy, the Japan Society of Obstetrics and Gynecology forbids its doctors to reveal the gender of a baby before then.

The predilection for daughters is strongest in Japanese women. A majority of Japanese men still prefer to have a boy if they have only one child, but most men want one child of each sex. This leads some observers to conclude that women's yen for girls may not translate into more female births since many men may not cooperate with the sex-selection regimen chosen by their wives.

Whether or not the girl craze produces more females, experts say that it is noteworthy as an indicator of profound social change that includes a national pension system that makes male offspring less essential in financially supporting their elderly parents, a weakening of the ancestral male-dominated family system, increasing individualism and the much improved socioeconomic status of women. But some people say that more parents want girls because life is no longer sweet for Japanese boys. To hear them tell it, hapless male tots are condemned to endure the take-no-prisoners Japanese educational system, followed by a life sentence as a faceless drone for Japan Inc.

Section IV

Japan's Jet Program:
A View From Within:

JET TEACHERS AND A FOUNDER EVALUATE TOKYO'S BID TO IMPORT DIVERSITY ON A MASSIVE SCALE

The earlier sections of this book focus on the views and attitudes of Japanese students. The following section turns the picture around. Here three young American women, all recent graduates of Mary Baldwin College, give their perspectives on teaching in Japanese primary and secondary schools as participants in the Japanese government's JET program.

The Japanese government inaugurated the Japan Exchange and Teaching (JET) program in 1987 in a dramatic effort to "internationalize" Japanese society. This regimen imposed from above, so typical of Tokyo's attempts to revolutionize Japan since the Meiji period (1868-1912), has grown into a massive government operation costing nearly a half-billion dollars a year and employing more than 6,000 young foreign nationals in public schools all over Japan. Thirteen years after the first JET teachers arrived in Tokyo, scholars are intensely debating both the rationale and the viability of the program. After studying the program both directly and indirectly for nearly a decade, I have come to the conclusion that despite its many problems and deficiencies, JET has brought meaningful contact between thousands of foreigners and millions of Japanese who might not otherwise have ever even spoken to a foreigner. On the other hand, the government's hope that JET would lead to improvements in the ability of Japanese to speak better English has not been realized.

The JET program has a remarkable historical precedent in the early Meiji period when approximately 3,000 "hired foreigners" (*oyatoi gaikokujin*) were employed by various governmental and private agencies to assist in Japan's early modernization. Since the Meiji period, however, Japan has sought to deal with the outside world through arm's length strategies. Japanese trading companies, for example, provide the expertise and contacts abroad for Japanese businessmen so that they don't have to deal with foreigners in any meaningful way. Today many Japanese have some interest and experience with the West, but they rarely if ever travel or study in the rest of Asia. Indeed, Japan's next-door neighbor Korea is about as alien for most Japanese as it is for most Americans. To this day foreigners are brought in to assist the Japanese develop in the modern world, but those same foreign workers (such as myself) are ignored socially. Many foreign teachers in Japan find their Japanese teacher colleagues to be cold and distant.

David L. McConnell, a College of Wooster (Ohio) anthropologist and Japanologist, analyzes Japan's dilemma in the mid-1980s:

Having completed one of the most dramatic economic turnarounds in recorded history, Japan nonetheless continues to suffer from an acute image problem within much of the international community…[Scholars note that] for all its overseas connections, Japan's intense feelings of isolation and exaggerated sense of uniqueness are increasingly criticized by the rest of the world as barriers to business and by Japanese themselves as embarrassing social handicaps incommensurate with Japan's growing status as a world economic leader. Thus, at a time when pluralist nations around the world are struggling to integrate their culturally diverse populations, Japan is under intense international pressure to solve the opposite problem: to "create diversity" and to acquaint its insulated people with foreigners at the level of face-to-face interaction.[33]

My greatest shock when teaching well-over 200 Japanese students was the very literal insularity and parochial state of their education and world views. Foreign writers often note that Japan remains a closed nation at heart and that ethnocentrism and xenophobia guide Japanese thinking. There is certainly a great deal of truth to these claims, but there are also many Japanese with an appreciation of the outside world, who genuinely promote international ties, and who seek ethnic diversity at home. The most severe test of the JET program is its ability to "chart a course between the sincere desire of Japanese to raise their status within the world community and the deep-seated sense of separateness still felt by many Japanese today."[34]

The JET program has many important goals, some stated and others implied. The clearest goal is to enhance the teaching of English in Japanese middle and high schools and to introduce it into primary schools. My experience with students in Kyoto showed the critical need for this step. A secondary goal is to create diversity in Japanese neighborhoods by placing younger Americans and other Westerners in schools throughout Japan. Today there are small foreign communities even in the remotest corners of Japan. A further goal is to enhance foreign understanding of Japanese society—to use JET to create better feelings for Japan among young people abroad.

---

[33]. David L. McConnell, *Importing Diversity: Inside Japan's Jet Program* (Berkeley:University of California Press,2000),p. ix.

[34]. Ibid., p. x

The greatest fault with the primary and secondary educational system in Japan is the almost complete emphasis placed on preparing students for college entrance exams. What are potentially the most valuable years for foreign language learning are totally wasted in the course of hour after dreary hour in the English classroom with Japanese teachers, most of whom drone away in Japanese explaining the grammar and pronunciation of a language that they themselves have hardly ever heard and certainly can't speak.

If JET teachers are supposed to help Japanese improve their English, their success has been limited. JET teachers are often assigned to three or four schools and they only appear in any given class only on occasion. These few visits to generally large classes provide limited benefits to individual students. Many JET instructors complain that they are used sparingly and that they waste much time every day sitting around writing letters and reading. They note that too often Japanese teachers are more concerned with covering points of grammar than with having native speakers in their classes. English learning in secondary schools has not measurably improved since the inception of JET, and Japanese rank low among all Asian nations in terms of scores on English tests like TOEFEL. JET has noticeably failed to improve English skills among young Japanese.

JET teachers, on the other hand, are having a positive effect in primary schools. Several experimental programs which I visited on several occasions in the city of Nagaoka in Niigata and elsewhere, have been developed to introduce English to first and second graders. JET teachers play games, sing songs, and give Halloween parties to excited youngsters who love mingling with the foreigners and learning basic English expressions. JET would do well to focus more of its attention in primary schools where children actually enjoy learning English and enjoy the company of young foreign teachers.

One of my former students and current JET teacher in Nagaoka, Tarah Blazek notes:

The third goal of creating greater appreciation and understanding of Japan among thousands of young foreigners is hard to measure. Some returnees pursue further studies about Japan and East Asia and enter careers or jobs that require an understanding of Japan and Asia. One returned school teacher regularly tells her primary school students about Japan and has many Japan-related projects. Returnees tell their friends and neighbors about Japan and often give talks and write articles. But it is harder to judge whether the program has improved foreign impressions of Japan.

At the very least JET has forced the integration of many foreigners with millions of Japanese who might never have met a foreigner otherwise. Virtually every Japanese student has had at least one encounter with a young foreign teacher in class and Japanese teachers have developed badly needed team-teaching skills. English learning in secondary schools has not measurably improved since the inception of JET, but the very presence of thousands of young foreign teachers in remote schools and neighborhoods may begin to reduce Japan's severe ethnocentrism and improve its international awareness and impressions of foreigners.

COMMENTARY OF JET PARTICIPANTS

Since the late 1980s well over twenty graduates from Mary Baldwin College have participated in JET. The following material includes an interview statement by JET-founder, Representative Otohiko Endo, and personal reflections by three former Mary Baldwin students who taught as JET instructors: Kate McDonald, Kristin Williams, and Susannah Courand.

OBSERVATIONS ON THE JET PROGRAM BY ONE OF ITS FOUNDERS:
Otohiko Endo

[Mr. Endo provided the following comments during an interview with this writer in July 1999 in his office at the Japanese Diet. Endo, a longtime member of the Soka Gakkai, was, until 2000, a Komeito Party member of Japan's Lower House of parliament representing a Tokyo district. Endo studied at Oxford University and was a ranking member of the Ministry of Foreign Affairs before launching a successful political career that has included a post as a junior-member of a Cabinet.]

We developed the idea for the JET program years ago when I was working in the Japanese Ministry of Foreign Affairs. We were increasingly aware of Japan's isolation from the outside world as well as the low-level of English education and ability in Japan. Even though Japan had become fully integrated in political and economic affairs throughout the world, there were small communities near Tokyo where residents had never seen a foreigner or had no real English ability.

Our goal in creating the JET program was to help increase Japan's communication with the outside world. We decided to bring in several thousand young, enthusiastic and well-educated English-speaking foreigners not only from England and North America, but also from other parts of the world including South and SE Asia and Australia. These young guests all teach in our schools, but their role is much more than that of teacher. When students meet and study with a foreign teacher, very often they lose their fear of foreigners. When JET teachers participate in community events, visit their Japanese neighbors and eat in local restaurants, everybody in the community has a chance to know them. And when several thousand JET teachers return to their native lands each year, they tell their families, friends and neighbors about Japan. In this way we can raise the level of intercultural understanding among between Japan and the outside world.

Many critics say that the JET program costs a great deal, but the tangible and intangible benefits are very real. [Soka Gakkai leader Daisaku] Ikeda has always urged us to open up ties between Japan and the outside world. The JET program is an excellent manifestation of Ikeda's teachings.

JET: A WELL-INTENTIONED PROGRAM WITH ROOM TO GROW
By Kate McDonald

[Kate McDonald graduated from Mary Baldwin College in 1999 with majors in English and Asian Studies (honors). She studied at Doshisha Women's College in 1997 and participated in the JET Program in 1999-2000. Her employment base was in Nagahama in Shiga Prefecture near Kyoto]

Having almost finished my year in Japan with the Japan Exchange and Teaching (JET) Programme, I am beginning to look forward to my return to the United States and the life that awaits me there. However, as the weather continues to improve, promising the coming of Spring and my departure in July, I have also begun to look back on the myriad experiences I have had here. It has undoubtedly been wonderful, and the decision to come to teach at a small junior high school in Nagahama, a city in the north of Shiga Prefecture, is one that I will never regret.

I truly believe that the JET Programme is a great organization which provides a fantastic opportunity for young people like me to live and work in Japan, but after working within the program for a year, I struggle to find more substance to it than that. The goal of the JET Program, as stated by the Council for Local and International Relations (CLAIR), is to promote international relations and increase pro-Japanese sentiments world-wide by bringing young people from thirty-six countries around the world to work in local boards of education and city halls, coach sports, or teach their native languages in elementary, junior high, and high schools. Unfortunately, the JET Programme misses the mark by a long shot.

When I read the *General Information Handbook* which all JET participants receive before coming to Japan, I noticed many of the articles and essays contained a disclaimer stating that because "every situation is different," the information contained within them might not be relevant for everyone entering the program. Throughout my year here, beginning before I even left for Japan at Pre-Departure Orientation in Washington, D.C., and continuing at Tokyo Orientation, and even now, at prefectural and even city meetings, that sentence, "Every situation is different," has been repeated ad nauseam. And if I had to name one cause for the ultimate failure of the JET Programme to meet the demands it puts on itself in its mission statement, I would have to say it again: Every situation is different.

There are no standards for guidelines regulating the placement, treatment, or use of JET participants, and in a country which works so hard to create the impression of uniformity, it is surprising that this is the case. Every detail of our jobs differs because we each must sign different contracts. CLAIR has a sample contract which it sends to all the host institutions, but the host institutions often change it, adding or removing clauses as they deem appropriate. The final contract which each participant signs does not necessarily have to be approved by CLAIR, and thus, CLAIR remains unaware of what each participant is told to do, allowed to do, or prevented from doing.

Admittedly, most of the changes are rather superficial—whether or not we can drive cars or motorbikes to work, for example. Others, such as sick leave and vacation day allowances, are ones of convenience. But some changes seem to unnecessarily open the door for abuse of the participants' positions within their schools and city halls. In my own contract, a clause under the list of duties I am expected to perform states that I must do anything my supervisor believes to be appropriate or of importance in accomplishing the goals of the JET Programme. While I know of no misuse or stretched interpretation of that particular clause, many JETs in the region are not pleased that it exists and are currently attempting to remove it. Such discrepancies are allowed because of the lack of supervision by CLAIR.

In addition to this, we are asked to commit to joining the JET Programme before we are given our placement information and asked to sign our contracts. Thus, the participants have already entered the program and are unable to withdraw without facing serious consequences when their host institutions present them with their contracts. They must agree with the conditions outlined because they simply have no other choice. The remedy to this–to have one contract that applies nationally and that is sent to the successful applicants with the acceptance letters–is one that would simplify and clarify the process for all.

Many of the problems with the program are the result of CLAIR being merely a placement agency for the JET Programme. While CLAIR attempts to stay involved by offering support services for JET participants and sending out newsletters, the actual employers are the host institutions–the city halls, local boards of education, and prefectural offices. CLAIR receives the list of successful applicants and then passes the names and applications along to the various institutions in need of new JET Programme Assistant Language Teachers (ALTs), Coordinators for International Relations (CIRs), and Sports Exchange Advisors (SEAs). Once the names and applications have left CLAIR's offices, the host institutions are fully responsible for the details of arranging for the JETs' arrival and everything which that involves. Because apartment rental, appliance purchases, and basic furnishing are taken care of on the local level by the cities or prefectures, there are huge variations in the standards of living for JETs.

Some of these differences are unavoidable; apartments in and around large cities will always be smaller and more expensive, and it is often possible to find a large house with low rent in the country. However, it does not stand to reason that some JETs are allowed cars, move into fully furnished apartments, or are located only a short ride from their schools or train stations while other JETs are not allowed to drive at all, must furnish their apartments themselves, or must ride their bikes more than half an hour to their schools or stations. The lack of uniformity in the living situation of JET participants is only one small example of the extent of diversity in our situations, and it is one which does not always have a large direct effect on the fulfillment of the program's mission statement. The kind of setting into which a JET enters, however, can affect his or her morale, which over time can influence his or her performance and attitude toward Japan.

These differences are not limited to the standard of living of each JET; they often reach into the work life as well. Again, this is an area over which CLAIR claims little control. There are many types of positions open for ALTs, and as with the contracts, the JET applicants do not know in which position they will be placed until after they have agreed to join the program. It is possible for one person to teach at only one school the entire time he or she is in Japan and for another participant to never visit the same school twice. ALTs may teach as many as twenty-three classes a week, more than most trained, full-time Japanese teachers, or as few as five classes a month.

For obvious reasons, these differences play a direct role in the success or failure of the JET. While ALTs who spend most of their time at one or two schools have a greater opportunity to positively influence English education and interact with their students, ALTs who visit many schools rarely teach more than their self-introductions. The ideal solution, of course would be to hire enough JET participants to have one in each school at least half-time. This, however, would cost a great deal of money and does not guarantee a high quality of performance as the standards for admission into the program would be lowered with a higher demand for applicants. Another option would be to only send JETs to schools who are able to use them properly.

Boredom at work is the most common complaint JETs make. Even the average ALT who teaches ten to fifteen hours a week at two or three schools has a lot of free time at work. JETs who are placed in agricultural,

technical, commercial, or disabled schools which do not place an emphasis on English education are those who seem to make this complaint most
often. Rarely are JETs given ideas on how to use their time at work, and
after a while, even the most motivated participants often fall into a routine
of e-mailing, letter writing, novel reading, or sleeping. For the money we
are paid–3,600,000 yen yearly–this is not a productive use of time.

When we are in the classroom, we are more often than not used
improperly and wind up feeling ineffective. This is perhaps the second
most common complaint of ALTs. The main cause from which most of
the problems stem is the lack of training for both ALTs and the Japanese
English Teachers) with whom they work. Only a small percentage of JETs
have actually taught before coming to Japan and a smaller number are
trained teachers. This inevitably causes problems initially as those with
little or no teaching experience adjust to their positions within the school.
Tokyo Orientation aims to help ease the transition into the classroom by
holding seminars on team-teaching and Japanese education, but again,
every situation is different, and it is difficult to cater to the specific needs
of each JET because of the discrepancies in each of our job descriptions.
It is not until we reach our schools that we are certain of what and with
whom we will teach.

Furthermore, the JTEs have rarely been trained to team teach and do
not know how to properly use their ALTs. As a result, the ALTs become
human tape recorders, worksheet designers, and game coordinators. Even
when the ALT is used properly and allowed to teach, he or she rarely sees
the class often enough to truly reinforce anything that was previously
taught. Despite the time ALTs spend encouraging natural conversation
and pronunciation practice in class, in classes without the ALT, too many
JTEs focus on the aspects found on the high school and college entrance
examinations, written English and listening practice.

Another problem with English education in Japan is that the Japanese
teachers themselves were not taught English well, and while many of them
can read or write English, they are unable to speak it. Even frequent

exposure to native English speakers in and out of the classroom is not enough to negate the improper grammar and pronunciation of the Japanese teachers, particularly when the students rarely regard the ALT as a real teacher. The only way for English education in Japan to truly improve is to adequately instruct the Japanese teachers in spoken English and convince them of the importance of verbal communication.

Admittedly, our job as participants of the JET Programme is supposed to be more about internationalization than about changing or improving the English programs in Japanese schools, but it is frustrating for many JETs, all of whom have undergraduate and sometimes even graduate degrees, to have their skills go unnoticed and unused. In addition, because of the high demand for JET participants and the program's desire to expose as many foreigners to Japan as possible, the ability to speak Japanese is not a requirement for ALTs. While ideally, the ALT should be able to communicate on some level with his or her students in the ALT's native language, the one he or she is teaching, this is seldom the case. Most discussions which take place between the ALT and the students outside of class tend to be in Japanese. Even in class, when the ALT is asked to speak about his or her home country, without the use of a lot of props and exaggerated gestures, the students quickly become uninterested and wait impatiently for a Japanese translation. In the cases when Japanese translation is unavailable, the cultural exchange that can take place is greatly limited.

Even though I have had some wonderful conversations with my students, in a mixture of Japanese and English, I still feel as though I have made little progress in really teaching them about my country, except perhaps about American pop culture. Among the ALTs with whom I have talked, this is a common occurrence. Only a handful of students in each school are willing to talk with their ALT on a regular basis, and the others seem to view him or her, not as a real human being, but as a great source of amusement, a role which can be fun for the ALT and students for a while, but which can also be limiting and discouraging after a long time spent at the school.

It is a great waste of time and money for local boards of education to hire foreigners only to have their skills and abilities as native English speakers go unused. It neither fosters international exchange nor improves English education. Instead, by altering the program to make it more uniform nationally and incorporating training programs for both JET participants and Japanese teachers, the JET Programme may very well achieve its goals and become more than a means by which foreigners can get paid for experiencing Japan.

THE VIEW FROM TANEGASHIMA
By Kristin Williams

[Kristin Williams, a 1997 graduate of Mary Baldwin College, minored in Asian Studies before entering JET in July, 1997. She returned to the US in 1999 and soon plans to seek an advanced graduate degree in Asian Studies]

When I tell Japanese where I spent my time in Japan, they invariably burst into laughter followed by, "Tanegashima? Why?" The JET Program sent me to an small (179 square miles) island four and a half hours south of Kyushu by ferry. Tanegashima is a beautiful,tranquil island rich with history, but it's not a major tourist destination. The miles of sandy beaches stay empty, although the current flowing from the South keeps the water warm even in the spring and fall. Tanegashima's claims to fame include a space center and the first muskets, rice cultivation, and sweet potato cultivation in Japan.

While in high school, I had lived on a Marine base in Japan for two years, but going back to live on my own between two sweet potato fields was an entirely different experience. Especially at first, I struggled with the language barrier combined with a sense of being cut off from everything familiar. There was a group of American engineers working at the space center during my first few months, but, not having a car at that point, I rarely got together with them or the 3 other foreign English teachers, none of whom lived in my town. Chances to see foreigners and speak English were rare and precious, so I appreciated the orientations, conferences, and the Japanese class that I attended as part of the JET Program. On the other hand, not speaking English is a great way to learn Japanese, and I became much more involved in the life of my town than I would otherwise have been.

I tried to use my time in Tanegashima to the fullest because there was so much I wanted to learn and so many people I wanted to befriend. I volunteered to teach two additional adult classes in my spare time, and I joined the local "Mama-san chorus" and a church. I visited the library often, reading, talking with students, and helping with the storytelling group which annually hosted a traveling children's theater troupe in addition to story-time activities for children and workshops. On two occasions, I guided foreign dignitaries around the island, explaining the itinerary, interpreting, and introducing the island's history. A couple times, I even translated letters found in bottles that washed up on the beach. When I found myself with free time at work, I studied Japanese, observed classes, or talked with colleagues. Singing karaoke, traveling, snorkeling, swimming, and walking made the two years pass quickly.

While on the JET Program, I taught English to children, adolescents, and adults. Since I was not the primary teacher in most classes, I had the opportunity to focus on speaking and using English. In one adult class, I began by going around the classroom, doing introductions and shaking hands. One man told me after class that he had never spoken English to a foreigner before, and he was delighted that he could. That my simplest efforts could have an impact was both a blessing to me and a great responsibility.

Children growing up in Tanegashima today have many more opportunities to speak English. Minamitane (South Tanegashima) Town has one junior high school and eight elementary schools, one in each village. I visited each elementary school three times a year. On my first visits, I was shocked at how small some were. One school had 21 students, 3 teachers, a principal and a vice principal. Even in this tiny school, there were computers and a swimming pool. Behind that particular school was a hill with a banana grove, a shrine, a shiitake mushroom garden, a tangerine grove, and tires to climb on during recess. This was hardly an average Japanese school, but the variety and quality of schools in the town surprised me as did the cheerful chaos of the junior high school.

After hearing of the strong discipline of Japanese schools, I did not expect to see my students hopping through windows and playing hide-and-seek in the halls. My Japanese colleagues assured me this was not a normal school, and I know schools in more populated areas are more strict. Still, one of the great things about JET is that it provides the opportunity to see aspects of Japan that tourists or television cameras may not.

Tanegashima has changed greatly in the past ten or twenty years. Many homes have satellite dishes but lack modern plumbing like flushing toilets and hot water. Only thirty years ago, cars and paved roads were so rare that my neighbors' marriage was forbidden at first because, living in different villages within the town, the bride's parents would have had to travel many hours to visit. When I was helping students translate speeches into English, one girl, Rena, asked me how to say "overblessed" in English. I asked her to explain, and she said that she believed that Japanese are too happy and too blessed materially. She felt she must leave Japan to share her happiness with people in other countries who were in need. Her passion for this idea convicted me because I have so much more than she who will probably never have the opportunity to go to college or travel to another country. The greatest learning experience for me was stepping outside of my culture to see others as neighbors and friends. I learned as much about my own culture as I did about Japanese culture, and learning the stories of individuals and the island's legends planted in me a desire to know more of the stories of my country and my family as well.

SURFING IN JAPAN
By Susannah Courand

[Susannah Courand, a 1998 Mary Baldwin graduate and Spanish major, spent two years in a small town near Nagaoka in Niigata]

Before actually arriving in Japan the only images I had were the bright lights and businessmen in dark suits packed on the trains of Tokyo. I could not have even begun to envision an industrial town in the heart of rice and snow country Japan which I currently call home. I had very limited knowledge of the history and culture of Japan, absolutely no Japanese language skills and not a clue about what to do with the bunch of Japanese Junior High School students that I was going to be teaching. Needless to say, I jumped into the JET program with blinders on. Now that my time here is soon to reach the year and a half mark, I look back and realize how much I have learned since I cluelessly stepped off the plane back in July of 1998. I accept the fact that I will never be too enlightened as to the Japanese way of doing things, as well as the language, but I am really happy that I have had a glimpse into this culture which has been closed for so long (and in many ways, still is).

What amazes me about this country is the fact that it is so modern and industrialized, yet its inhabitants continue to steadfastly retain their traditions and cultural heritage. Things that are Japanese are clearly defined as such: Japanese noodles, Japanese tea ceremony, Japanese flower arranging. Unfortunately for a struggling outsider like myself, the common assumption seems to be that since I am not Japanese, I probably cannot: use chopsticks, eat sushi, speak Japanese or generally master anything Japanese. This can be very discouraging for the foreign resident struggling to find a place in this society. Constant subtle reminders about being a foreigner (and therefore semi non-functioning in Japan) can very quickly lead to extreme feelings of isolation and culture shock. On the other hand, because we are different, foreigners achieve an almost celebrity status.

People are very interested in our daily lives. Experiences such as being appointed honorary fire chief for the day are countless and make me realize what unique existence I lead while living here. Many foreign residents I have talked to in Japan seem to experience similar episodes of extreme ups and downs, so in effect we are always riding the culture shock wave, sometimes it is cresting and other times, well, crashing.

When the wave is up, I feel like my job has a purpose and that my time in Japan is being wisely spent. When I first started teaching here, I often wondered why I was teaching English to students who don't want to learn it and may not ever need it. If the wave is up, it is easy to remember back to my trip to Thailand helping some Japanese tourists. Almost everyone in Thailand speaks English, particularly anyone making money from tourists. Since the tourists couldn't speak English, I helped them, trying to act as a translator with my limited Japanese. I have come to realize that, for better or for worse, English is becoming a universal language. If my students do decide to travel outside Japan without taking the stereotypical Japanese tour (complete with Japanese tour guides, stops at Japanese restaurants and only associating with other compatriots), it would be helpful for them to be able to speak a little English.

As I am an assistant teacher, I teach with a Japanese English teacher at all times. The responsibility of discipline and teaching textbook grammar falls on the Japanese teacher; I try to make the students communicative and interested in English by devising fun activities using English conversation. On good days, I like to be the assistant. It is very exciting to come up with a lesson plan that the students enjoy and it is encouraging that the students generally look forward to my visits to the class.

Aside from work, life in the JET program couldn't be better. I realize that a vacation is never too far away and the weekends are like vacations in that I can jump in my car and visit a new place. I marvel at the fact that I can go anywhere in the world with little consideration of money and only slight strategic thought as to how to most efficiently use my paid leave to get the most vacation days. I feel lucky that I have gotten to meet so many people from English-speaking countries outside of America. Through my friends on this program, I have learned so much about places such as England, Australia, New Zealand, Scotland and even the great state of Alaska (when asked, my friend claims that her nationality is Alaskan, maybe I should start saying mine is New Jersian to eliminate the which part question that always ensues). It is during this cresting period that I don't want to leave the life I have here.

I can understand how some people who come here with the intention of staying temporarily end up establishing a permanent life here. In fact, I myself was firm on my decision to leave up until it came time to sign the paper. This year I know will definitely leave in July, although sometimes I wonder why.

It is during the crashing period of culture shock that I am reminded of the difficulty of life in Japan. The thing about culture shock that I have found is that if you are in a bad state, it is hard to identify why. You blame isolated incidents, yourself, Japan, winter, etc. It is easy to forget this continuous cycle that we are on and in fact, depression may be setting in right on schedule (we were actually given a chart which maps out our culture shock level according to time spent here). This must be one of the few situations where a person can go through a whole day and night and not even talk to a single person.

I think of the JETs who cannot speak much Japanese and live in rural towns with no English-speaking people around. As teachers in Japan are very busy, sometimes it is difficult for them to make time to speak with us. Not communicating with other people, or communicating on such a basic level due to limited language ability, is very lonely experience for some JETs. In that situation, most seem to either learn Japanese and assimilate as fast and as much as possible, or get out as soon as possible. And while being ignored and isolated is no fun at all, the aforementioned celebrity status can also lead to, or worsen, a crashing period. When I first arrived here, I felt honored to be invited into people's houses and be considered the guest of honor at various events. Towards the end of last year, I began realizing that many of these people are studying English and pay good money for lessons and that by hanging out with me they get to practice English for free. Others just want to hang out with foreigners. Both of these reasons for being included are fine to a degree, but when your family, many friends and culture are thousands of miles away, you really start to long for real friendships and being liked for who you are rather than the fact that you are a native English speaker. It begins to be very important that the people you spend your free time with are interested in you instead of your country or your language and grammar points. I guess this is why here in rural Japan, an organized JET function is never too far off.

I have found that the best way to get through these bad spells is to realize that while I may be used to it now, I am still living in a society very different from my own. Everything I do is twice as hard as it would be at home, from mailing a package to holding a conversation. This constant extra stress is bound to affect us to some point and it is only natural that we feel the effects from time to time.

Despite my complaints, this has been a great learning experience for me. I have learned a lot about patience, cultural sensitivity and life abroad. People have really been generous and kind to me from the moment I arrived. It has been very interesting to see a culture operating differently from my own, yet very smoothly. Many pains are taken to promote group harmony, known here as *wa*. I have come to appreciate cultural traditions such as *omiyage* (exchange of gifts. It seemed like an expensive and time consuming tradition at first, but I have come to look forward to giving away presents after returning from a trip or visiting someone in the house. In more formal relationships, it is a good ice breaker and I think its overall purpose is just to promote good vibes. Many of our aggressive western ways seem very barbaric compared to the levels of civility here. Patience is a big difference that I see among the foreigners living here and the Japanese. Although Japan is thought to be an efficient country, everything you do involves a big process, usually some paperwork, and lots of waiting. Being brought up among the complaining populous of the New York City area, it amazes me how people here will wait silently in line for almost anything. This is particularly annoying at fast food establishments, where the people actually want to eat the food and are not just eating it for lack of options or time, as many people in the US do.

You can end up waiting for 30 minutes while they package' Bigu Macus' in three different bags. While my American blood pressure is rising and I am biting my tongue not to complain, and everyone else is happily waiting their turn, I realize how much healthier it is to be patient. At restaurants, people order what is on the menu, how the restaurant chooses to serve it. I used to try to get my meal served exactly how I wanted it, with this substituted for that, but I gradually have seen how demanding that must seem from a Japanese perspective and have learned to just point to the picture like everyone else.

I have started to become more and more accustomed to doing things and seeing things the Japanese way. When I think about leaving, I know I will lose my celebrity status upon returning Although I sometimes look forward to moving back to my familiar culture, I realize it may be difficult to re-assimilate.

ENGLISH FOR LITTLE KIDS
By Tarah Blazek

Younger kids learn foreign languages very well, but when they get older, it is much more difficult. It would be much better if the Mombusho would begin teaching English seriously as early as first grade.

Over the past three years I have taught in a variety of primary schools in the Nagaoka area. Whereas my middle school students often showed little interest in English and were often intimidated working with a foreign teacher, my elementary kids loved our English classes.

One of our best days was a Halloween exercise where Dr. Metraux and I put on a big party. We gave out candy, sang songs, and had the students trick-or-treating all over the school. It was all part of a pilot project by the Japanese government to see if English teaching in elementary school works. I can tell you! IT WORKS!!

— — — — — —

JET has grown into an immense program that has the potential to bring revolutionary change to Japanese society, but a host of problems have turned JET as it exists today into a largely ineffective and hugely expensive concept that needs restructuring and rethinking if it is to realize its potential.

JET does bring together foreigners and Japanese in a manner that was almost inconceivable before 1987. I visited former students Susannah Courand and Tarah Blazek in the small city of Nagaoka several times between 1998 and 2000. When I visited Nagaoka in the 1970s, it was a very isolated city hours away from Tokyo by train with virtually no foreign population.

Today Nagaoka is closely linked to Tokyo by the super-express *Shinkansen* railway and is home to over two dozen JET teachers who teach in local schools and live in their neighborhood. Every school has at least one JET teacher which means that every student has had some contact with a foreigner, which is quite a change for the people of rural Japan. There are even foreign teachers in the small mountain villages in this "Snow Country" quarter of Japan.

JET teachers live separately in neighborhoods scattered around the area and very often have contacts with some of their neighbors. Every JET I visited, however lonely she might be, had at least some meaningful contact with locals. There is now a substantial foreign community in Nagaoka, however transient, and the locals seem quite used to having so many foreigners in their midst.

The problem for JET comes in the actual teaching experience. The entrance exam system at each level of Japanese education requires one to pass a difficult written test, and Japanese education is extremely test-oriented. Teachers must prepare the students rigidly for the test and must follow a daily schedule, which means that there is little or no time in many cases for the JET teacher who focuses mainly on conversational skills, which are NOT a part of any entrance exam. The tragedy therefore is that so many of the JET teachers, who are already spread very thin between classes and schools, are in fact very under-utilized and therefore forced to sit day after day in offices with really nothing to do. The most successful application of JET appears to be in elementary schools where the students are more receptive to English lessons and there is less pressure to memorize everything for tests.

JET has a lot of promise for the future, but more teachers and local educators must figure out better ways to use the teachers. Virtually all of my Japanese college students had had some contact with JET teachers, but most deemed that connection to have been quite useless.

Conclusion

One of the most striking features of female college students in Japan today is their high degree of passivity. A small number of these students do stand out from the crowd in the sense that they have very clear goals in life and demonstrate clear attributes of leadership. But it is far more common to encounter young women who have great difficulty in making decisions for themselves, who wait for directions from authority figures and who have a clear picture of how they want their lives to develop beyond the scope of a safe marriage and a job.

The media, both Japanese and American, declares incessantly that this young generation of Japanese is very different from that of its parents and grand parents. In some respects, this is true. More women go to college, get better jobs and stay working longer, and now delay marriage until age thirty. The number of women seeking professional careers in areas outside of teaching and nursing is increasing slowly and the divorce rate is soaring. More young women are living on their own after college, supporting themselves. Traditional *omiai* are out and love marriages are in. Young men and women determine their own relationships and decide when and where they will marry. Fewer young wives will live with their in-laws. Many young women dye their hair outrageously and wear very hip clothes and boots.

These changes are very real and pronounced, but they mask the very deep sense of passivity that still remains. Male barriers to good jobs out of college and to meaningful job tracks and promotions are very real, but young women create their own barriers because very few of them are willing to even consider professions or meaningful careers. There are very few women lawyers and scientists because only small numbers of women actually prepare for careers in these areas. Opportunities exist for women who are willing to make the sacrifices, work hard, and challenge or work around the male-dominated networks that exist in each area. There are more than a few very successful female lawyers, accountants, scientists and politicians, but each of these people had a sense of ambition and willingness to work hard. Japan is still a male-dominated and to some degree even a "male chauvinistic" society, but opportunities do exist for women who choose to take advantage of them.

The young college women that I taught in Kyoto, however, exhibited a deep sense of passivity concerning their lives. Very few had any career or professional goals and close to eighty percent perceived of their lives around marriage. They judged motherhood to be the most noble and important profession of all. Several said that they wanted long-term jobs that would provide them with good incomes and a sense of independence, but absolutely nobody talked about careers or professions. There was a lot of talk about the dream job, that of an airline stewardess who could travel around the world for three years before settling in for a more mundane life.

One can blame Japan's educational system, including women's colleges, for part of this problem. Although Japanese women are just as well educated as men in the "basics," they are rarely told that they have the ability and right to plan and develop their lives as they see fit. This tendency is certainly perpetuated in women's colleges where women are trained for jobs, but are not trained in the professions and for any leadership role in society. One can study English, other languages, music, Japanese, food science and a few basic courses in business and computers, but there is NOTHING in the natural sciences, math, and very few social science courses. Graduate courses only perpetuate this cycle.

When I challenged several of my more advanced students to look far beyond positions as airline stewardesses, a couple did launch aggressive job searches involving smaller, rapidly growing companies in scientific / hi-tech areas. To their surprise and delight, both of them succeeded. I urged another to transfer out of the women's college and into the main co-ed university and, to her surprise, her application was accepted.

The idea that women have the potential to achieve whatever they want was a constant theme in all of my classes, but the students paid more attention when I brought in current or former American or Canadian students to talk about opportunities and careers for women. The biggest hit was Megumi Okura, a graduate of the school who had spent her junior year as a transfer student at Mary Baldwin College and who had returned to the U.S. to teach Japanese at MBC and to pursue a graduate degree in Japanese pedagogy at Columbia University. After she spoke to my classes about her own successful efforts to develop a career, masses of students surrounded her asking how she was able to "make it."

One of Prof. Okura's answers surprised them: "self-confidence." She explained that the main thing that inhibits young Japanese women today is a lack of self-confidence. Early in her college career she decided that she wanted to travel to the U.S. for a year and to study at an American college even though her knowledge of English was very poor. After graduating from college, she was determined to teach at an American college as a T.A.

or instructor while getting an MA in how to teach Japanese. Again, her iron will and her total confidence in herself allowed her to achieve all of her goals in less than three years.

Prof. Okura said that a vast majority of young Japanese women lack confidence because they have never been told by their parents or taught in school that they could make strong decisions about their futures and that they could pursue a professional life. Large corporations perpetuate this tendency by quite often taking even talented women graduates of prestige universities and trying to encourage them into a "women's track" in contrast to the male's "executive track." A few talented women who do "make it" do have the confidence to overcome these obstacles, but very few of them are actual graduates of women's colleges.

The methodology of education is also at fault. Japanese women get superb training in the basics of reading and writing, but the old cliché, that Japanese cannot think for themselves does hold true for many young women. There is no real attempt to challenge the mind, dispute authority, take adventures in virgin territory. Female students are much too timid to even ask questions in class. It took nearly 8 months of teaching in Japan to convince students that it was ok to discuss their opinions in the open.

I was most successful in my English conversation classes where students were obliged to make 2-3 minute speeches in English presenting their views on a major social, cultural or political issue chosen each week (early on they could use notes, but later they had to speak on their own without notes). Their terror in speaking in public was at first intense, but later in the year virtually all of the students had overcome their fears and strode to the center of the room with a sense of confidence. They also learned to express very diverse opinions very well.

The vast quantity of courses they take at once is also a major fault. A freshman taking fourteen to sixteen courses is simply overwhelmed. She arrives at school early and leaves late, is continually exhausted, and has no time to think or study. They are often unable to provide a full list of the courses that they are taking. They have little respect for their courses because the value of each course to their academic careers is minimal at best. Their official transcripts look good and the grading is easy, but everything is hollow. Two years of Chinese study, for example, include only about 50 ninety-minute classes and no time to study between classes. It is thus no small wonder that young Japanese are so poor at languages today despite transcripts that say they had many years of study.

The sections in this book on society and politics and war and peace demonstrate that Japanese women have very clear opinions on issues and that they are very able to express their own opinions and to debate issues openly with each other if given the opportunity. They enjoy and greatly profit from such exercises which they called "mind liberating," but they are never given a chance. Teachers bark boring lectures their way in a most insulting and relentless manner and the students sit there, staring out the window or closing their minds to the unheard and unwelcome words. There are, of course, a few professors who do engage their students in open discussion and creative thought, but, unfortunately, they are a distinct minority. The students are thoroughly bored with their studies and long for the moment when they can get their degree and hopefully find a job that will give them some degree of freedom and independence before they decide to get married. A degree is a ticket to freedom and is not a guarantee that the graduate has mastered much in her academic career.

It is striking that one's grades do not really matter as long as one passes. Any grade between 80-100 was an A, 70-79 a B, and 60-69 a C. Below 60 was failing. Since most courses are prescribed and failing means that one must repeat the year-long course before liberation at graduation, everybody strove to pass the courses. A few students, especially in my junior advanced writing and American Studies classes, really cared about learning and doing well and came to class on a regular basis, but others only came on occasion and their submission of assigned work was spotty at best.

Virtually everybody passes in this system, but employers rarely if ever inquire about a person's grades and performance in school. The simple act of graduation is basically all any employer cares about which removes any real incentive to do well in school. And, as previously noted, seniors are rarely in class because they are so busy looking for jobs. This means, sadly, that the senior year and those courses taken during that time are often a sham.

Young women could very well play an important leadership role in the future of their nation, but it is clear that this will not happen under the current system. Even if corporate Japan were suddenly to open its executive tracks to young women, a most unlikely scenario, they would be unprepared and generally unwilling to take up the challenge. But unless women are brought into the system quickly and are trained and strongly encouraged to assume leadership roles on a massive scale, Japan's future as a major world power is at best bleak.

Japan is a nation without any meaningful natural resources. Its highly skilled, well-educated, and hard working people have always been its greatest resource, its hope and its salvation. Diminishing numbers of skilled workers and leaders endanger this critical resource, but young women could do much to reverse this trend.

www.ingramcontent.com/pod-product-compliance
Lightning Source LLC
Chambersburg PA
CBHW020253290526
45784CB00003B/1229